Local Business Marketing

Making the Phone Ring for Small Businesses Everywhere

Other Titles by Connie Ragen Green

Local Business Marketing

Making the Phone Ring for Small Businesses Everywhere

Connie Ragen Green

Copyright © 2019 by Hunter's Moon Publishing

ISBN Paperback: 978-1-937988-46-3
ISBN eBook: 978-1-937988-47-0

Hunter's Moon Publishing
http://HuntersMoonPublishing.com

Interior Design by Shawn Hansen
Cover Design by Shawn Hansen

Dedication

This book is for Claes. In 2006 he patiently observed as I fumbled about with websites, blogs, and marketing. He then became the first person to hear me talk about marketing for small businesses. He was also the first one to trust me to market for him and make his phone ring. Without his belief in what was possible for him when I leveraged the power of the internet to grow his business none of what followed, including this book and twenty others would have been possible.

And for Emelie Melissa, our beautiful girl. Just yesterday you held Winnie the Pooh close to your heart and today you are bravely stepping forth to embark on your own grownup adventure. May all of your dreams come true and the people you encounter along your path continue to surprise and amaze you.

Contents

Forward

Connie Ragen Green saved my life. Not literally, for things were not ever so bad that I contemplated ending it all. But figuratively yes, she saved my life because she saved my business.

I started my business right out of college. I earned my D.C. - Doctor of Chiropractic - in June of 1982 and opened my first office less than two months later. I was living in Pennsylvania at that time. A year later I met the woman who would become my wife. Her family lived in southern California so we packed up and headed west.

Starting out in a new city didn't bother me, but over the years many new chiropractors began opening offices within a few miles of my practice and this made for stiff competition. Over the years there were ups and downs but it wasn't until 2008 that I was afraid I was going to have to close my doors for good. My business was down to forty percent of what it had been for the previous three years and I had to let two of my employees go. That was tough.

One night my wife and I were out for dinner with friends and they suggested I join Rotary. They told me this was a service organization that helped people in need, locally and also around the world. I was at a low point right then and agreed to give Rotary a chance. There was a club not far from my office and the following week I showed up for lunch at the restaurant where they held their meetings.

The first person I met was Connie. She smiled and shook my hand and brought me over to meet the club president. Then she guided me to the registration table where she told the secretary that I was her guest. I hadn't even thought about paying for my lunch. This was a new world and I did not know how it worked.

She saved me a seat at the table where she was sitting, introduced me to a couple of people, and then disappeared to the other side of the room so I could make my own introduction with the people who were coming in for the meeting.

After the invocation, Pledge of Allegiance, and a song there were announcements, fines, and lunch. It was during this time when I asked Connie what she did. I don't recall everything she said because the only part I heard was "and I help local businesses to make their phone ring."

That's when I interrupted her and asked if she could help a chiropractor. I was at the point where I thought that perhaps my profession could not be helped.

After the meeting Connie came to my office and the next evening she was invited to my house for dinner. She explained everything she could do for me, offered two different plans, and I signed up for the less expensive one. Money was tight and I was a little skeptical of how this type of marketing worked.

She set up a simple website for me, had me join an online forum primarily for real estate agents but also for professionals and those in the trades. She also had me sign up for Twitter and that made me raise my eyebrows a bit. But I was beginning to trust Connie and had few other options. Newspaper advertising was too expensive, as were radio spots and those mailers that had small flyers from thirty of more businesses and were sent out every month.

My wife and I agreed that having Connie do for us what she was already doing for several other businesses made the most sense at that time. We had shaken hands on a six month verbal agreement and I hoped this would make the phone ring like she promised.

It got worse before it got better because the economy took an even steeper downturn that spring. That next month was the lowest in revenue I had experienced in almost twenty years. Then it happened. My receptionist sent me a text asking me to come back to the office right after the Rotary meeting. Yes, I was now going every week. I didn't have a client until four o'clock but I did as Nancy asked and returned to the office.

She was standing up when I came in and didn't say a word. She pressed the button to start playing back messages and there were three of them. One person said they read my blog post about the benefits of chiropractic for stress reduction and wanted to schedule an appointment. Another had found me on Twitter and was ready to come in. The third one said she was new to the area and wanted to begin working with a chiropractor and when she went to Google my name was everywhere.

Nancy had not called any of these people back to schedule appointments because Connie had recommended I do it personally. I spoke with each person, learned more about their situation, and booked the appointments. I had never had three new patients in one day in all my years and it felt good.

That night I called Connie to thank her. She was so kind and gracious and gave me all the credit for being a professional she was proud to represent. She asked if she could stop by the office the next day to make some short videos and of course I said yes.

Connie marketed for me for two years before training one of my daughters to take over for her. That daughter was in college full time and only needed to work a few hours each week for spending money, thanks to my increased earnings. My son learned how to take over when my daughter got married and now my wife and I are grandparents. These days I have a virtual assistant who does this for me. I sure never thought I'd be saying I had a virtual assistant but it works out very well.

What Connie did for me and for many other business owners is nothing short of magic and a kind of miracle. When she says she makes the phone ring that is just a small part of what she makes happen. She was able to eliminate my competition by making me stand out as someone different in my profession. Her ideas are big and most of them work better than she probably thought they would. With her help I am now known for my chiropractic services and my volunteer work in my community.

Every time someone tells me they found me on the internet I silently say a thank you to Connie. So when she asked me to write something for this book I couldn't say no. She even got my wife to agree to lend a hand if I couldn't think of something to write but that didn't happen. If you have the good fortune to learn from her, jump at it and do what she says. Thank you, Connie for saving my business so I could provide for my family.

~ Daniel Sullivan, DC.

Preface

It was time for me to write this book. After marketing successfully for a family member in 2006, and then two business owners from my local Rotary Club by early 2007, and finally taking on several more clients later that year it was evident this was a worthwhile endeavor. But my true reason for writing this book at this point in time is that I see a trend, or actually a few problematic trends that I would like to become a part of the solution to solving.

These trends involve small businesses once again having to struggle to keep their doors open. The reasons for this are political for the most part, in my opinion. It shouldn't be this way.

Small businesses are the backbone of the American economy. Without them, everyone suffers. Later on I will present some facts and figures around this topic; for now I am speaking from the heart.

As I began outlining this book I thought back to my earliest days in the work force. I have shared some of these stories throughout this book as a way to exemplify my experiences in a relevant manner.

My first official job came at age fourteen when I was hired to be a hostess at the Uncle John's Pancake House a few blocks from my home in Miami, Florida. This restaurant had just opened when the manager agreed to allow me to work a few hours each weekend.

Everyone involved benefited from that business opening during the summer of 1969. The manager was my neighbor. I found out later he had lost his previous job several months earlier and his wife and two children were about to go live with his in-laws when he was hired on. One of the cooks had recently returned from Viet Nam with something we now know as PTSD (post-traumatic stress disorder) and was having a difficult time adjusting back into society. He used to thank me for being nice and always saying hello and smiling when I saw him. This job enabled me to buy school clothes at the end of the summer, something I had never experienced up until that time and also to help my mother with the rent and the groceries.

Three very different people, three very similar stories of how a job helped each of us to move forward with our lives. A year later and we would all be on to new life experiences and working in different jobs in various locations. Again, jobs that would make a difference in our lives.

Uncle John's Pancake House was always busy, especially on the weekends. This type of restaurant was new to the American landscape and people flocked to it to experience a meal where they could choose the food items they wanted from a six page menu that showed photos of food in living color. A hostess would seat you and ask you for your drink order. A waitress would wait patiently while each member of your party told her what they wanted, and sometimes in great detail with specific requests. A cook prepared your food so that it was all fresh and hot when it was delivered to your table a short time later. A busboy scooped up the dishes, glasses, and flatware, wiping the table clean so the next party could be seated. The cashier took your money and handed you a receipt. If you hadn't done so already, one in your group would make their way back to the table to leave a fifteen percent tip.

Yes, it cost more than what it would to eat at home. But then, the idea of going "out" to eat was a novel one to most working class Americans during the 1960s. It never would have occurred to me that this restaurant would have to close its doors if enough customers ceased to come through these doors on a regular basis.

Uncle John's was located along Biscayne Boulevard, the main street that ran south all the way to downtown Miami and north until Dade County turned into Broward County. Everything was exactly as it should be for them to attract the right customers into their large parking lots with oversized spaces for cars and trucks and campers of all shapes and sizes. The food was good; there was a wide selection of items on the menu to satisfy every member of the family; the prices were reasonable; and the employees were friendly.

Yet in 1991 they shut their doors for good after that section of Miami underwent major growth and a change in the demographics. The building that had housed the pancake house fell into disrepair, the land and building were purchased soon after, and almost immediately the improvements were razed to make room for two smaller restaurants. One was a Brazilian steak house and the other one served Ethiopian food. Today there sits a Starbucks drive-thru at the opposite end of the parking lot and this area is now going through gentrification.

When I came to the realization in 2006 that I could help small businesses to stay in business it was as if I had come full circle. I couldn't wait to leave the work force and become an entrepreneur, yet I knew as well as anyone what a job can mean to someone. I figured if I could help as many business owners as possible to keep their doors open then it was as if I were personally helping people like myself to have the experience of earning an income and conforming to a job on their way to the life they desired.

In 2010 I began teaching these principles to more people through an online course called "How to Market for Small Business." Two years later I began teaching local business marketing to people who attended my two and three day live marketing events and workshops. In 2015 I took on a joint venture partner, Ron Tester to help teach this topic in greater detail. Ron has run a successful home healthcare agency in Texas for more than twenty years and was the perfect choice as someone who can bring more depth to a subject we both feel so strongly about. He and I both consult with business owners as they meet the challenges of developing and running a thriving business during this decade and beyond.

I have done my best to share as much detail as possible with you here and to not leave out anything you may encounter later. Please contact me if you have additional questions, have an interest in the online course, or would like to arrange a consultation. LinkedIn may be best; I'm Connie Ragen Green there.

Introduction

This book is structured in what I consider to be a logical way that allows the reader to move effortlessly through the information I have included. It is written in five sections, and with two or three chapters within each section. Even though each chapter stands on its own and is not dependent upon your having read the chapters that came before it, it is preferable for you to read from beginning to end if you intend to have great success with your small business marketing goals.

There is a method to my madness with these sections and chapters that may not be apparent to you until you are half of the way through the book or even further along. Please trust my instincts here and it will all make sense by the end.

In the first section I first discuss the history of marketing and advertising. Without knowing where we came from in these areas you will be at a disadvantage as you seek out your own path. Then I bring us up to modern times where we learn that some of the strategies through the centuries still ring true. In the third chapter I share everything you need to know to truly leverage the power of the internet with virtual storytelling, websites, and email marketing.

The second section takes us into the world of branding, getting to know your target audience, and exceeding your potential as you grow you business.

Creating a solid and sustainable business growth plan and incorporating marketing into your life comprise the third section. I also introduce a concept I continue to use and benefit from, becoming a local celebrity. This is sure to change your thoughts and perceptions as to how you can grow your local business more easily.

I include my Eight-Pronged Approach to Local Business Marketing at the beginning of the fourth section. As tempting as it may be to skip over to that right now, I implore you to work your way through the preceding sections and chapters first.

Then I discuss attracting the right clients for you and your business, the all important goal of making the phone ring, and how to incorporate social media into your marketing efforts using the strategies that makes sense for you.

The fifth section is where I discuss what could be next for you after you have read this book and implemented what I have included. You may then wish to market for other small businesses and/or teach marketing to other business owners, both of which will be rewarding as you give back to others.

I will leave you to make your decisions as to how you will move forward. Please know that I want to hear from you regarding what your experiences and results are during and after reading this book.

Section One – What Is Marketing?

"Marketing is really just about sharing your passion."
~ Michael Hyatt

I did not understand marketing during the twenty years I worked as a real estate broker and residential appraiser. Even though I was required to take two college level courses in this area in order to sit for the broker's exam in California this topic was confusing and vague to me over the years. Certainly I did not understand its importance in determining the level of success I would be able to achieve.

It wasn't until I started my business as an online entrepreneur in 2006 that the pieces began to fit together in my realm of understanding and consciousness. At some point early on I came to the realization that life would have been much easier if I had employed even a few marketing strategies on a regular basis instead of waiting for the phone to ring all on its own.

The history of marketing is a fascinating one. It's a journey of discovery, where necessity is at once the mother of invention and the cog in the wheel. Over the centuries marketing has been a graceful and delicate dance, a focused and deliberate walk on a tightrope, and a deep dive to the bottom of the sea and up to the surface again, waves splashing and salt water in your nose. The power of marketing can be intoxicating and dangerous. It's the juxtaposition of an abstract concept that is so very simple alongside one that is complicated and delves into the recesses of the human mind. The pillars of tradition, honor, discipline and excellence are juxtaposed with the students' four pillars of travesty, horror, decadence, and aplomb.

The future of marketing is likely to be a story as riveting as any told by the greatest minds of generations to come.

While this is not intended to be a textbook on marketing, or an all inclusive study of this topic, having a basic understanding of the concepts and principles that have evolved since the beginning of time and those that continue to thrive will serve you well as you market for your own business or one owned by someone else.

The History of Marketing and Advertising

"The radio craze will die out in time."
~ Thomas Edison, American Inventor, in 1922

Even though marketing in one form or another has been around since the beginning of time, let's begin our journey of investigation just before the beginning of the Industrial Revolution.

As you may recall from studying about history in school at different grade levels, the Industrial Revolution period spanned the late 18th century and lasted long into the 19th century. It was a time of rapid social change in the world and was motivated by innovations in the scientific and technological industries. Agricultural societies became more industrialized and urban. The transcontinental railroad, the cotton gin, electricity and other inventions permanently changed society. People left farms in droves and headed to the growing cities where they believed life would be easier. It was also more complicated due to the advances that were being made in almost every industry and facet of life.

Here is a timeline of what occurred during the period just before the beginning of the Industrial Revolution and moving into the prime years where modern marketing got its roots:

What is now referred to as the Simple Trade Era began around the beginning of time and lasted into the mid 1800s. Everything that was available during this period was either hand created or harvested by hand. Exploration was the main focus of the economy at the time, and so was trade. Everything was in limited supply because of the fact that most things were handmade and harvested. It was also a time when basic commodities ruled people's lives. Households would only produce what they consumed and very little was wasted.

But first, let's look more closely at something that would change the world forever. The year was 1450 and the printing press had been invented by Gutenberg. His innovative metal, movable type not only led to the mass production of print products, but more importantly to marketing pieces such as brochures, fliers and direct mail.

In our world of rapid change it's difficult to imagine it taking almost three hundred years for magazines to make their first appearance after the invention of Gutenberg's press. This would become a future vehicle for advertising and niche marketing that first occurred during the 1730s, when the definition shifted to being "a place or position suited to or intended for the character, capabilities, status, etc. of a person or thing."

In 1836, the first paid ad showed up in a French newspaper, marking the true beginning of a long partnership between modern media and marketing.

In 1839, business marketing took a major hit as posters displayed on private property in London were banned.

In 1864, the telegraph was used for ad space, marking the beginning of unsolicited mass spam, a fundamental of business marketing right to this very day. We find it funny they used the word spam way back then, but that's exactly what it was as an advertisement going out to people's hardware without them requesting it. This was like a text message being sent a hundred fifty years before society embraced this form of communication.

The year 1867 marked the first known use of billboards via rented space for ads.

The 1880s saw trademarks start being used for branding purposes.

I hope you find this walk through history to be as fascinating as I do. Deconstructing the past leads to a more robust and productive future, in my opinion.

It was during the Industrial Revolution that purchasing goods began to be easier for a consumer than for he or she to make things themselves. The focus here was on serving the masses. Mass production created many industries engaged in the same endeavor to serve the needs of a growing consumer market. The infrastructure for public and private transportation as well as mass media took hold. It created a need for producers to find better ways to develop products customers needed and a more sophisticated approach to informing them about these commodities that were now available to all.

We then moved into the Sales era, which ushered in the complex era of fierce competition. This would change the world forever as businesses could no longer easily sell their mass made products to end users. It increasingly became more difficult for companies to communicate in a way that would lead to sales of their products to consumers. This era is where we see the concept of marketing as it is today emerge. Companies had to aggressively promote their products and persuade consumers in order to sell products. Competition increased. The need to increase selling by using marketing techniques became an essential part of being competitive. The ability to develop a unique brand and appropriately market it grew in value. This was the beginning of advertising, which would increase the quality of what was produced and created as well as the manner in which each product was introduced and presented to the world.

Basic Marketing Concepts Come to Light

As savvy businessmen start to understand the power of marketing, basic concepts are established and explored, laying the roots for modern business marketing in the 1900s.

In 1905, a course called "The Marketing of Products" was first offered at the University of Pennsylvania.

1908 brought about the opening of the world-famous Harvard Business School, proclaiming to the world that "business" as an industry was now here to stay.

The 1910s saw terms being defined, classifications being determined and conceptualization being actualized, bringing marketing to life in vivid color. What I wouldn't give to have been a fly on the wall during this period of history.

During the 1920s, the basic principles of marketing began to be integrated across all mediums, leading to the advent of radio advertising in 1922 and eventually, marketing theory and narrow specialization being developed during the 1930s.

The 1940s saw new demands being placed on marketers by a transforming business sector. This led to a more scientific approach towards business marketing being developed, culminating in the invention of the electronic computer (forerunner of today's marketing), though it wouldn't be used for marketing for some time. I am of the opinion that this decade was one of the most powerful in terms of laying the groundwork for what was to transpire through the end of the twentieth century.

Radio and Television Change Everything

Even though most people today spend more time surfing the internet and using mobile devices than they do listening to the radio or watching television, it's important to understand how these two broadcast media platforms came to be and laid the foundation for what we enjoy today and sometimes take for granted.

To this day radio and television continue to reach a wider audience in real time than print media. The radio and television commercials fall under the category of mass marketing as the national as well as global audience can be reached through it. Organizations such as the Federal Trade Commission (FTC) are in the background, monitoring the commercials on television and radio. This ensures that the advertisers are not making any false claims to lure consumers to buy their products.

In 1900, Brazilian priest Roberto Landell de Moura transmitted the human voice wirelessly. According to the newspaper Jornal do Comercio, on June 10, 1900 de Moura conducted his first public experiment on June 3, 1900, with journalists in attendance, along with the General Consul of Great Britain, C.P. Lupton, in São Paulo, Brazil, for a distance of approximately five miles (about 8 km). The end points of transmission and reception were Alto de Santana and Paulista Avenue.

One year after that experiment took place, de Moura received his first patent from the Brazilian government. It was described as "equipment for the purpose of phonetic transmissions through space, land and water elements at a distance with or without the use of wires." Four months later, knowing that his invention had real value, he left Brazil for the United States with the intent of patenting the machine at the U.S. Patent Office in Washington, D.C.

Having few resources, de Moura had to rely on friends to push his project forward. Despite great difficulty, three patents were awarded: "The Wave Transmitter" (October 11, 1904), which is the precursor of today's radio transceiver; "The Wireless Telephone" and the "Wireless Telegraph", both dated November 22, 1904.

The next advancement was the vacuum tube detector, invented by Westinghouse engineers. On Christmas Eve 1906, Reginald Fessenden used a synchronous rotary-spark transmitter for the first radio program broadcast, from Ocean Bluff-Brant Rock, Massachusetts. Ships at sea heard a broadcast that included Fessenden playing "O Holy Night" on the violin and reading a passage from the New Testament of the Bible. This was, for all intents and purposes, the first transmission of what is now known as amplitude modulation or AM radio.

Nathan Beverly Stubblefield was an American inventor who received widespread attention when he gave a series of public demonstrations of a battery-operated wireless telephone, which could be transported to different locations and used on mobile platforms such as boats. In 1908 he received a U.S. patent for a wireless telephone system that used magnetic induction. Stubblefield was unsuccessful in commercializing his inventions.

In June 1912 the British Marconi Company opened the world's first purpose-built radio factory at New Street Works in Chelmsford, England.

The first radio news program was broadcast August 31, 1920 by station 8MK in Detroit, Michigan, which survives to this day as all-news format station WWJ under the ownership of the CBS television network. The first college radio station began broadcasting on October 14, 1920 from Union College, Schenectady, New York under the personal call letters of Wendell King, an African-American student at the school.

That month 2ADD (renamed WRUC in 1947), aired what is believed to be the first public entertainment broadcast in the United States, a series of Thursday night concerts initially heard within a 100-mile (160 km) radius and later for a 1,000-mile (1,600 km) radius. In November 1920, it aired the first broadcast of a sporting event. At 9 pm on August 27, 1920, Sociedad Radio Argentina aired a live performance of Richard Wagner's opera Parsifal from the Coliseo Theater in downtown Buenos Aires. Only about twenty homes in the city had receivers to tune in this radio program. Meanwhile, regular entertainment broadcasts commenced in 1922 from the Marconi Research Centre at Writtle, England.

Sports broadcasting began at this time as well, including the college football on radio broadcast of a 1921 West Virginia vs. Pittsburgh football game.

Mechanical televisions started appearing in the early 1800s. These involved scanning images mechanically and then transmitting those images onto a screen. Compared to electronic televisions, they were extremely rudimentary.

The world's first electronic television was created in 1927 by a 21 year old inventor named Philo Taylor Farnsworth. He lived in a house without electricity until he was fourteen and starting in high school. He then began to think of a system that could capture moving images, transform those images into code, and then move those images along radio waves to different devices.

Farnsworth was miles ahead of any mechanical television system invented to-date. Farnsworth's system captured moving images using a beam of electrons (basically, a primitive camera).

The first image ever transmitted by television was a simple line. Later, Farnsworth would famously transmit a dollar sign using his television after a prospective investor asked "When are we going to see some dollars in this thing, Farnsworth?" The first image of a human ever televised was that of Farnsworth's wife, Pem later that year.

Between 1926 and 1931, mechanical television inventors continued to tweak and test their creations. However, they were all doomed to be obsolete in comparison to modern electrical televisions: by 1934, all TVs had been converted into the electronic system.

The idea of broadcasting was a new one in the 1940s. The first TV ad popped up on screens in 1941 in America – probably a lot later than you'd imagine. Before the Brooklyn Dodgers and the Philadelphia Phillies played each other, viewers saw a brief commercial for Bulova clocks and watches. Such a small moment set the precedent for the next seventy years.

These days we use what is referred to as "narrow" casting with podcasting and cable television. Narrowcasting, also referred to as niche marketing, is defined as the dissemination of information (usually via Internet, radio, newspaper, magazine, or television) to a narrow audience; not to the broader public at large.

The next time you watch television or listen to the radio remember that you are witnessing the results of a great and innovative history.

Marketing and Advertising Perceptions Based on Broadcasting

Let's first define advertising before we continue any further. Advertising is a marketing communication that employs an openly sponsored, non-personal message to promote or sell a product, service or idea. Sponsors of advertising are typically businesses wishing to promote their products or services. Advertising is differentiated from public relations in that an advertiser pays for and has control over the message. It differs from personal selling in that the message is non-personal, i.e., not directed to any particular individual. Advertising is communicated through various mass media, including traditional media such as newspapers, magazines, television, radio, outdoor advertising or direct mail; and new media such as search results, blogs, social media, websites or text messages. The actual presentation of the message in a medium is referred to as an advertisement, or "ad" or "advert" for short.

Since its very first beginnings, which are thought to date back to steel carvings made by the ancient Egyptians, advertising has constantly had to adapt and change to suit new mediums and an increasingly savvy audience.

Egyptians used papyrus to make sales messages and wall posters. Commercial messages and political campaign displays have been found in the ruins of Pompeii and ancient Arabia. In ancient Greece and ancient Rome lost and found advertising on papyrus was common. Wall or rock painting for commercial advertising is another manifestation of an ancient advertising form, which is present to this day in many parts of Asia, Africa, and South America. The tradition of wall painting can be traced back to Indian rock art paintings. These date back to 4000 BC.

In ancient China, the earliest advertising known was oral, as recorded in the Classic of Poetry (11th to 7th centuries BC) of bamboo flutes played to sell confectionery. Advertisement usually takes in the form of calligraphic signboards and inked papers. A copper printing plate dated back to the Song dynasty used to print posters in the form of a square sheet of paper with a rabbit logo with "Jinan Liu's Fine Needle Shop" and "We buy high-quality steel rods and make fine-quality needles, to be ready for use at home in no time" written above and below is considered the world's earliest identified printed advertising medium.

In Europe, as the towns and cities of the Middle Ages began to grow, and the general population was unable to read even the simplest and most common words, instead of signs that read "cobbler", "miller", "tailor", or "blacksmith", images associated with their trade would be used such as a boot, a suit, a hat, a clock, a diamond, a horseshoe, a candle or even a bag of flour. Fruits and vegetables were sold in the city square from the backs of carts and wagons and their proprietors used town criers, also known as street callers to announce their whereabouts. The first compilation of such advertisements was gathered in "Les Crieries de Paris", a thirteenth-century poem by Guillaume de la Villeneuve.

In the 18th century advertisements started to appear in weekly newspapers in England. These early print advertisements were used mainly to promote books and newspapers, which became increasingly affordable with advances in the printing press; and medicines, which were increasingly sought after. However, false advertising and so-called "quack" advertisements quickly became a problem, which ushered in legislation aimed at the regulation of advertising content.

Moving Into the 19th Century

As the economy expanded across the world during the early 19th century, advertising grew alongside it in new and unique ways. In the United States, the success of this advertising format eventually led to the growth of mail-order advertising. That is a story in itself, but not as relevant to our overall topic so I will not discuss it in any detail.

In June 1836, French newspaper La Presse was the first to include paid advertising in its pages, allowing it to lower its price, extend its readership and increase its profitability and the formula was soon copied by all titles. Around 1840, Volney B. Palmer established the roots of the modern day advertising agency in Philadelphia. In 1842 Palmer bought large amounts of space in various newspapers at a discounted rate then resold the space at higher rates to advertisers. The actual ad – the copy, layout, and artwork – was still prepared by the company wishing to advertise; in effect, Palmer was a space broker. The situation changed when the first full-service advertising agency of N.W. Ayer & Son was founded in 1869 in Philadelphia. Ayer & Son offered to plan, create, and execute complete advertising campaigns for its customers. By 1900 the advertising agency had become the focal point of creative planning, and advertising was firmly established as a profession. Around the same time, in France, Charles-Louis Havas extended the services of his news agency, Havas to include advertisement brokerage, making it the first French group to organize. At first, agencies were brokers for advertisement space in newspapers.

The 20th Century Arrives

Thomas J. Barratt of London has been called "the father of modern advertising". Working for the Pears Soap Company, Barratt created an effective advertising campaign for the company products, which involved the use of targeted slogans, images and phrases. One of his slogans was,

"Good morning. Have you used Pears' soap?"

This was famous in its day and even far into the following century.

Barratt introduced many of the crucial ideas that lie behind successful advertising and these were widely circulated in his day. He constantly stressed the importance of a strong and exclusive brand image for Pears and of emphasizing the product's availability through saturation campaigns. He also understood the importance of constantly reevaluating the market for changing tastes and mores, stating in 1907 that "tastes change, fashions change, and the advertiser has to change with them. An idea that was effective a generation ago would fall flat, stale, and unprofitable if presented to the public today. Not that the idea of today is always better than the older idea, but it is different – it hits the present taste."

A print advertisement for the 11th edition of the Encyclopedia Britannica appeared in the 1913 issue of the National Geographic magazine. This was a bold move at the time that paid off with an increase in sales of both the magazine and the encyclopedias. Britannia had previously used direct marketing and door-to-door sales to sell its product.

Advertising increased dramatically throughout the United States as industrialization expanded the supply of manufactured products. It was 2.5 percent of gross domestic product (GDP) in the States during 1919, and it averaged 2.2 percent of GDP between that and 2007. This number declined dramatically during the Great Recession years of 2007 and 2012.

Consumer spending increased substantially and that led to the increase in productivity. This then contributed to the development of mass marketing designed to influence the population's economic behavior on a larger scale. Throughout the 1910s and 1920s, the majority of advertisers in the U.S. adopted the doctrine that human instincts could be sublimated - targeted and harnessed into a higher level of desire to purchase commodities. Edward Bernays, a nephew of Sigmund Freud, became associated with the method and is sometimes called the founder of modern advertising and public relations. Bernays used his training in psychology to develop concepts around the behavior of man based on motives and actions.

Modern advertising originated with the techniques introduced with tobacco advertising in the 1920s, and most significantly with the campaigns of Edward Bernays, considered the founder of modern,

"Madison Avenue" advertising.

But there's been one medium that's had a bigger impact on advertising than anything before it.

The internet. The wonderful World Wide Web. Science fiction turned into our daily reality. The world made smaller and smaller each day.

The internet has revolutionized advertising in the most astounding way. Not only has it changed the way ads are broadcast, but it has also changed the way consumers act towards them.

So now that we've familiarized ourselves with the history of marketing and advertising, how does this give us better insight into how we will market our own small business and those owned by others in the twenty-first century?

Modern Day Marketing Principles

"Give them quality. That is the best kind of advertising."
~ Milton Hershey

Studying the history of something we wish to excel in is a wonderful way to avoid reliving past mistakes and to embrace the principles and concepts that have endured the test of time. Marketing is no different. If you wish to market your own small business, as well as help local businesses in your city or town, this is where you begin to develop the mindset of a modern day marketer using the best of traditional styles and methods.

And just as I picture the ancient Egyptians taking the time to get to know one another in their local marketplace before they asked someone to buy from them, it is the same in the twenty-first century; it's all about relationships.

In my experience over the past decade and a half I have come to the conclusion that there must be a focus in three primary areas for you to experience the greatest success as a business owner and marketer.

These are:

- Building meaningful, strategic relationships
- Positioning yourself as an expert on your topic
- Networking to gain local celebrity status

I will deconstruct each of these so you may better understand the inherent power and potential when you focus on improving what you are already doing in these areas.

It will already make sense to you to build relationships with others in your local community and beyond. But if you are going about this in a random, haphazard way you will benefit from what I am sharing with you here.

Make a list of your current "circles of influence." These will include groups you are a part of on a regular basis such as service organizations, trade associations, your Chamber of Commerce, the PTA at your child's school, the church or other religious group you attend, the ballet or symphony or little theatre, a club or gym you belong to, and any other group you spend time with on a regular basis, even if that is only once or twice a year.

You will have at least an informal list of the current members of each one of these, along with some contact information for each person. Look through these lists and from them create a second list of the people you have communicated with in person, by phone, or through email during the past year. What is the percentage of connection you come up with?

When I first did this exercise in 2005 my "circles of influence" included the teachers and administrators at my school, my local Board of Realtors, and the church I attended occasionally. My percentage of connection with these three groups was less than one half of one percent. I simply did not understand the value of connecting with more of the people who were a part of groups I was already involved in because we shared a common interest.

A year later, after I had left my job as a classroom teacher and begun my business as an entrepreneur, author, and marketer my numbers had quadrupled; within three years my percentage of connection had grown by leaps and bounds and my new business was thriving. I was also new to the community where I had relocated to and did not know a soul when I first arrived so this was quite the accomplishment for me.

I achieved this goal by making it a focus and a priority to build meaningful, strategic relationships from within my current circles of influence, and to add more people and groups to my circles over time.

This was possible even though I am an introvert, was starting for the first time at the age of fifty, and did not have a mentor to guide me during my first year of challenging myself to grow my business. You can do the same if you make this part of the process a priority in your life. You may even find it to be fun and something you look forward to every day. Having a mentor will allow you to accelerate your growth exponentially.

First, look for service organizations in your city or in a city or town not too far away. These might include Rotary, Elk's, Lion's, Kiwanis, Zonta, and others you may or may not be familiar with because of the work they do. These groups are not religious or political in nature and they each have causes they work towards, both locally and internationally.

I chose Rotary as my first group because the members were kind and welcoming when I visited a few times over a period of several months. Soon I learned they were involved in local work helping veterans in a variety of ways. Their "big picture" goals included bringing fresh water to people in Africa and South America by digging wells and installing other types of water treatment systems within villages and also working to eradicate polio from the planet by going in to remote villages and administering the vaccine. I joined in December of 2006, several years before Warren Buffet and Bill and Melinda Gates would donate hundreds of millions of dollars to the Rotary Foundation and challenged each Rotarian to match their gift in the fight to end polio.

I will admit I was intimidated at first to be socializing and volunteering side by side in the community with such an esteemed group of people. Once I settled in to the rhythm of serving others in need while also having the opportunity to create and grow relationships with these new people in my life I felt like one of the group.

I began working with a mentor about a year after becoming a Rotarian and he taught me how to build more meaningful and strategic relationships from within the group of about eighty people.

Here is what I learned and have continued to implement over all this time when it comes to building meaningful and strategic relationships:

- Reach out to members of your "circle(s) of influence" one at a time at first. The way I did this was to keep a printed copy of the membership list and contact information on my desk next to my computer. Every day I would call up someone on that list and ask them a question, even if I already knew the answer to it. This allowed me to have three minutes of their undivided attention so they could hear my voice and be reminded that I was a new member of the club.

- After you have made your way through the list - it took me about three weeks the first time - make arrangements to connect with one or two of the members in person. I heard several of the Rotarians at my table one day talking about going to the local Elk's Lodge on Friday evening and I asked them what would be going on there. They told me it was the Friday night dinner and that I should come. I did. I sat at their table and met their spouses and friends. I stayed for almost three hours and made new friends while also being able to share more about myself than I ever could at a weekly Rotary Club meeting. One of the women at our table invited me to check out a women's business group called Zonta by attending their fundraiser the following week. I did. This was so much fun and I was beginning to build new relationships with people I liked and with whom I had something in common. I wondered why I had never done this in my life before now.
- After each encounter with new people and groups I went home and wrote down their names and what the group was focused on in the community and beyond. A year later I joined as an Elk, a non-profit in the United States dedicated to helping veterans from all wars and conflicts, as well as children born with major health issues. The following year I joined Zonta, an international service organization devoted to the advancement of women throughout the world. Soon people were calling me for various reasons, including asking me to join them in a volunteer opportunity and also to find out more about my business.

The strategy of positioning yourself as an expert could actually have come first in my list of three strategies, but I started from where I was at the time and did not feel like I would be considered an expert in the beginning. This was simply my perception and had no basis in reality. You may choose to reverse the order of these first two strategies or leave them as I have presented them here in order to achieve your goals.

I was writing every day and publishing my articles on my blogs and also on the article directories that existed at that time on the internet. When I began talking about this with my new friends and connections they were quite excited. Soon they referred to me as an author and entrepreneur and gave me credit for being much further along than I actually was at that point in time.

That was when I discovered that smart, successful people were very different from the people I had chosen to spend time with during most of my adult life. Instead of discouraging me from pursuing my goals and testing the waters with my newfound skills, these people actually encouraged me to explore the possibilities of what I was learning and doing each day. They treated me as though I had already become the person I so wanted to be. This made me feel like I could do almost anything I set my mind to do when it came to writing and building my online business as an entrepreneur.

Each Wednesday at my Rotary Club meeting I sat at a different table for lunch. This was for the purpose of getting to know more people in our group and sharing the details of what I was working on that week with them. I vowed at that time to be careful about who I spent time with in the future and not to allow negativity into my personal space ever again. I was empowered!

At the beginning of 2004, right at the time I was transforming my life as a classroom teacher and real estate broker/residential appraiser I had read a new book by Susan Scott, entitled Fierce Conversations: Achieving Success at Work and in Life One Conversation at a Time. This book was instrumental in helping me to better communicate with others and to allow them to view me in a whole new light.

Beginning at the school I was teaching at during that year, where I was so unhappy and felt misunderstood I began the process of upgrading my image and the perception others had of me. I did this one conversation at a time, whether it was with another teacher, a parent, or one of the administrators. The results manifested quickly. Within a month one of the teachers told me the principal had said something positive about me in a meeting I was not a part of, and soon after this woman was saying nice things to my face. And I do not mean she was complimenting me on my clothing or hairstyle; she was actually telling me and the other teachers what an excellent job I was doing at school with my lessons, teaching style, classroom management, and test results from the students in my classes. I stood up straight and tall and took my place at the table of respect.

Nothing had changed. It was simply that I was doing a much better job of communicating with the others and sharing bits and pieces of what I was doing as a teacher. The approach was one of "this worked in my class when we were getting started with the new algebra unit and maybe it would be effective for your students as well" and was generous and giving on my part without asking for anything from them in return.

At one point I printed out a few copies of how I was teaching narrative writing, based on something already included in the teacher's manual and left them on the counter in the teachers' lunch room. One of the teachers asked me what it was and I said that this worksheet was so helpful to me when I was getting the kids started I wanted to print out some extra copies for anyone else who needed them. To my knowledge no one ever figured out they already had access to this information.

I went from being perceived as another teacher struggling to get through the curriculum to someone who honestly wanted to be a helpful team player. Becoming a resource to my co-workers was beneficial to everyone, including me.

At lunch with my fellow Rotarians I had one conversation at a time to let them know what I was working on and how it could perhaps be helpful to them in their businesses. They in turn became my biggest fans, recommending me first as a speaker on the topics of content creation and marketing and social media marketing, and then as a marketer who could help local business owners make their phones ring.

The first taker was a Farmer's Insurance agent who needed more business. I was already doing this for a family member who had started a handyman service right around the same time as I had moved to my new community and started my online business. I used what was working for his business and adapted it to the insurance business, expanding my experience, knowledge, and expertise in the process. Being completely honest with him made it an adventure for both of us and his phone began to ring more regularly.

My new business model was now bringing in more income than I ever could have imagined and my services were in high demand. I was proud of what I was able to do for my clients. Years later they would share with me that they would have had to close their doors during the recession if it hadn't been for me. Grown men brought almost to tears while telling me their stories of struggle turned into triumph.

The next step and the third strategy in my marketing system was to get more people in my new community of over two hundred thousand residents to find out what I was doing and to connect with me, both in person and on the internet.

Networking to gain local celebrity status was more of a challenge, but only because I was finding my way and blazing new trails for my business. How could I become known in the community when I was new to the area and just finding my way as an entrepreneur and author?

The answer came soon after I put the question out to God and the universe. I was asked to appear on the local radio station to talk about Rotary's upcoming fundraiser. The interviewer began by asking me a little about myself.

During the previous few months I had been joining the local Chamber of Commerce for their monthly mixer. My goal each time was to meet as many people as possible during the ninety minutes I had set aside for this purpose every month and to tell them what I did so I could refine my "elevator" pitch and develop a brand around what I was doing in my business. After each encounter I would ask them if they understood what I did. In the beginning the answer was "no" and I kept changing my words and my story and my examples until the first person said "yes" and asked me a question that showed me they did understand.

So when the man at the radio station asked me what I did I sat up straight and tall in my chair and said,

"You know how someone opens a business and is excited to serve others with their products and services? Sometimes they are challenged with bringing in customers and making sales. I work closely with these local business owners to help them get their message out to the right people and to make their phone ring."

By the time I got home that evening my email inbox and answering service had blown up. Many people had heard me on the radio and wanted my help. And it wasn't only business owners who wanted to speak with me. There were people from various walks of life who were seeking out my help with writing, setting up websites, social media, and networking. We were in the early stages of the Great Recession, though none of us knew it at that time.

I sent a press release with the title "Santa Clarita Woman Helps Small Businesses with Marketing and Making the Phone Ring." Then I waited a day to call the local newspaper and ask them if they would write something about me and what I was doing.

This brought recognition to me, my Rotary Club, and to two of the clients I was marketing for at the time. I had launched myself as a person of interest in the community and as what I referred to as a "local celebrity."

In 2007 the Rotary International magazine contacted me about a project I had written about at one of our local elementary schools. I was not directly involved with this project and decided to share it far and wide to see just how far it could go. The magazine ended up doing a four page spread about this project and even used two of the photographs I had taken at the school. In the fifty years the Rotary Club in Santa Clarita had been in existence they had never once been mentioned in the magazine. A year later we were mentioned again and this time it was based on an article I had published on the topic of mentoring within service organizations. With a circulation of about 1.2 million readers worldwide this was quite a boost to our reputation as a club that got things done.

This led to a variety of opportunities for me, including an invitation from the Chamber of Commerce to accompany about forty small business owners to China for three weeks in November of 2008. The trip had been arranged by community leaders as a way to explore the economic and political climate in Asia as our own economy entered what would eventually be known as the Great Recession. I stood in the center of Tiananmen Square on Election Day and witnessed the reaction of the Chinese people when our new President (Barak Obama) was announced.

Our group floated down the Yangtze River in a bamboo and fiberglass boat that gave us a three hundred and sixty five degree view of our surroundings. This is the third longest river in the world, and the longest to flow within one country.

Upon my return I was invited to speak at two local marketing events, to the home of the Mayor for a fundraiser, and to speak at the Rotary District Conference in Los Angeles. This was an incredible opportunity for me to build my business right in my own backyard, while simultaneously doing the same thing on the internet.

Over this past decade I have taken full advantage of my celebrity status in Santa Clarita in terms of growing my own business, volunteering at many locations and with various non-profits and service organizations, and in assisting even more business owners to make their phones ring off the hook.

When our local community college opened a Veteran's Center and began offering a program to help returning veterans start their own business I was invited to speak to them about entrepreneurship.

Almost five years ago I was asked to write a column in the local newspaper on entrepreneurship and I continue to write for them to this day. They are also marketing clients of mine.

In 2012 I began living part-time in Santa Barbara, a gorgeous community about eighty miles (130 km) from Santa Clarita. It sits along the Pacific Ocean and allows me to breathe. I continue to go back and forth between these two cities but will eventually make my home full time in Santa Barbara.

I had become an accidental celebrity in Santa Clarita all those years ago and wondered if I could do the same thing on purpose in my new city. Yes, everything I am sharing with you here will work anywhere. Use my three strategies of building meaningful, strategic relationships, positioning yourself as an expert on your topic, and then focus on creating a celebrity status for yourself that will catapult your standing in the community.

You can accomplish the same thing I have done for yourself, your business, and for anyone whose business you are helping with marketing. And remember to serve others first as a primary focus and goal. Now let's move on to a discussion of how the internet has changed the way we market forever and why this medium is one that has far greater capabilities than have been imagined.

Leveraging the Power of the Internet

"The Internet is becoming the town square for the global village of tomorrow."
~ Bill Gates

Websites for Everyone

My first website was one I created for and with my middle school students during 1997. I set it up using Netscape Navigator Gold, which featured a WYSIWYG (what you see is what you get) HTML (Hyper Text Markup Language) editor. What this meant was that I could add text and even simple images and they would automatically save so that anyone with an internet connection, wherever they were in the world could view what I had published.

At some point I wondered whether anyone was seeing what I was adding to this site, but I wondered no longer when a representative from the Walt Disney Company contacted me regarding an image of a Dalmatian puppy I had used. It turned out to be a copyrighted image from the film 101 Dalmatians. I took it down promptly and learned an important lesson in the process.

By 2003 websites was become notably more sophisticated and businesses went from having nothing online or perhaps something very rudimentary to being able to hire one of the companies popping up everywhere to set up a site for them. I hired one of these companies that had been contracted by the Board of Realtors I belonged to and had them set up a site that was professionally designed.

That website was beautiful. It emitted heavenly sounds when you scrolled across the tabs and links with your mouse. The images of homes and scenery at the top rotated every ten seconds, fading in and out rhythmically.

Because I was a licensed broker and a member of the Multiple Listing Service the site had an area where visitors could do their own search for properties that were for sale. They would type in their criteria, such as the number of bedrooms or bathrooms, the location, and the price range and the results would be shown to them on one of my aesthetically pleasing pages.

Yes, it was a beautiful website but it never earned me any money or brought me new clients. It was what later became known as a "brochure" site. Lots of bells and whistles but no results.

During this period almost all websites were created using HTML, the Hyper Text Markup Language I referred to above. I learned how to use something developed my Microsoft called Front Page that allowed me to create simple web pages without having to write any code. That was way beyond the scope of what I was able to grasp and apply and not something I wanted to learn.

Around this time a platform called WordPress was becoming more popular. WordPress had been released on May 27, 2003, by its founders, Matt Mullenweg and Mike Little and was a free and open-source content management system (CMS) based on PHP & MySQL. I know this sounds very technical but it is my belief that we must know something about where WordPress came from to more fully appreciate where it is today.

When I came online in 2006 I took a close look at WordPress and decided that I did not have the technical skills to make use of this tool. I did not wish to learn these skills to be able to use this platform for myself or for others I would be assisting with their marketing.

Instead, I turned to a website platform known as Typepad for ease of use. It had originally been released in October of 2003 and had everything I wanted and needed in order to share what I was doing with the world via the internet. Typepad was co-founded by author and marketer Seth Godin and is a part of Six Apart's Movable Type Platform. It has since been purchased by an East Coast conglomerate.

During the first eighteen months I was online the world of technology made a huge shift, and even huge organizations like Time and the Huffington Post began using WordPress for its versatility and ease of use with something called themes and plugins.

Website Themes

WordPress users may install and switch among different themes with the click of the mouse. Themes allow users to change the look as well as the functionality of a website without even looking at the core code or the site content. It is in effect the "skin" of a website.

Every WordPress website requires at least one theme to be present and every theme should be designed using WordPress standards. These include structured PHP, valid HTML (Hypertext Markup Language), and also Cascading Style Sheets (CSS). Themes may be directly installed using the WordPress "Appearance" administration tool in the dashboard, or by using theme folders that may be copied directly into the themes directory, for example via FTP. The PHP, HTML and CSS found in themes can be selectively modified to alter theme behavior, or a theme can be a "child" theme which inherits its settings from another theme and selectively overrides features.

WordPress themes are classified into two categories: premium and free. Many of the free themes are listed in the WordPress.org theme directory, and premium themes are available to be purchased from many commercial marketplaces and from individual WordPress developers. A user may also create and develop their own custom themes. I continue to recommend using a free theme until you are further along with your site and require more choices and options to achieve your goals.

The Beginning of Plugins

The architecture of the WordPress plugin allows for users to extend the features and functionality of a website or blog. As of February 2019, WordPress.org has 54,402 plugins available, each of which offers custom functions and features. These enable users to tailor their sites to their specific needs. However, this does not include the plethora of premium plugins that are available (almost two thousand as of this writing) which may not be listed in the WordPress.org repository. These customizations range from membership sites, search engine optimization, client portals used to display private information to logged in users, content management systems, to content displaying features, such as the addition of widgets and navigation bars.

You must stay abreast of changes and updates to all available plugins or they may not function properly or may not function at all. This could also lay your site open to vulnerabilities from hackers. Most plugins are available through WordPress themselves, either via downloading them and installing the files manually via FTP or through the WordPress dashboard. However, many third parties offer plugins through their own websites, many of which are paid packages such as the membership plugin I referred to above.

I followed the trend and moved to WordPress in 2007 and have never looked back.

These days almost everyone has a website or at least a web presence. If you have a business or market for business owners this is the first topic you will address with them. I continue to find that most of them are using a template site of one kind or another. These are sold to business owners as a part of a package of digital products and services and are touted as being the best thing since sliced bread. They are not.

Templates lack the ability to be indexed on a deep level, making your SEO (search engine optimization) efforts difficult at best and futile in many cases. Whereas WordPress has the capability to publish your words immediately and have them indexed within minutes the majority of the time, templates simply store your words and publish them as a part of the original content.

WordPress is a CMS (content management system) that is second to none when it comes to website functionality. It can also be set up easily and is free with your hosting account. You only need to purchase a domain name (.com is preferred) in order to begin.

Setting Up a WordPress Website

There is a huge misconception and overall confusion when I tell people that WordPress is free. Yes, it's free and can be installed very easily, with the hosting account you will pay for in order to do this. The confusion arises when people Google for this information and come upon the WordPress.com site. That is not the place to set up your site!

Instead, sign up for a hosting account that will charge you by the month or annually for your account. Reach out to me if you need a current recommendation. This space has changed dramatically through the years and I do not want to go into a long explanation of what has occurred.

From within your hosting account you are able to do a one-click install of WordPress to set up as many sites as you want and need.

Then you will visit WordPress.org to learn more about the myriad of themes and plugins that are available to you at no cost and the technical information and details about each one, including the developer and the compatibility with your version of WordPress. It is of the utmost importance that you make yourself aware of what is current in this space.

Virtual Storytelling

Growing up I had neighbors my family spent lots of time with on a regular basis. Their son was a year younger than me and we became best friends very quickly. He had a pesky little sister who loved tagging along everywhere we went.

One day said little sister interrupted my mother in the middle of her sharing one of her myriad of stories and asked,

"Why do you have so many stories?"

My mother didn't skip a beat in answering,

"As you get older you'll also have lots of stories to tell."

I remember vividly the looks on the faces of these family members; the mother, father, and all four children seldom told a story to share about anything.

So perhaps storytelling is in my blood and that's why I took to this method as a marketing strategy so quickly.

In the "real" world where we connect with people face to face we typically hear their stories and learn about their background and experiences from them personally, even if it isn't natural for them to share such details in this way. On the internet people seldom meet in person and the stories are told through webinars and other presentations, interviews, blog posts, press releases, books, and social media.

What this means for you as a small business owner or someone marketing for local businesses is that your story will more than likely not be told unless you make the effort to tell it.

In the fall of 2008 I attended a marketing event in Los Angeles. It was a two hour drive for me and I parked in the almost full parking lot and went in to find the conference room. As I approached this area I observed several groups of people standing in circles they had casually formed and talking about the topic of this conference, online marketing.

Not knowing anyone there, I moved closer to a group that was talking about a woman who was an up and comer in this world. She had been a teacher prior to coming online and was now blogging, creating information products, and mentoring others on how to follow in her footsteps to achieve similar results. I was mesmerized by the stories they were sharing and vowed to somehow connect with this fascinating woman, until I finally realized they were talking about me!

I took a few steps forward and whispered something to one of the men on the periphery of the circle about what time they might open the door so we could go inside. At that moment someone recognized my voice from the teleseminars I was hosting each week and exclaimed "It's Connie Ragen Green!"

This was a milestone in my career and memorable for a variety of reasons. The most important of these was the fact that I was standing out from the crowd of competitors in the world of online marketing primarily because my story was compelling and one that resonated with those newer to entrepreneurship.

Think about your "story" as you tell it to others. What do you share? Which parts of your story are too private and personal to share with others? How can your story inspire, motivate, and encourage someone to do business with you?

My Story

My story includes something I refer to as "before, after, after." It consists of three parts. "Before" is the story of what my life was like before I came online in 2006. I was working as a classroom teacher in the inner city section of Los Angeles and also working simultaneously as a real estate broker and residential appraiser.

I was exhausted from spending six or seven days a week earning a living so that I could own my own home and provide for my aging mother. Then I went through cancer, not once but twice, as well as a serious work injury. It was during this period that I began to look for a solution to my situation. My prayer became:

"Please God; I need a way to make a living from home, from my bedroom if necessary in order to meet all of my financial obligations with grace and ease."

The answer came when I attended a conference and received a leather case filled with interviews of authors, inventors, and entrepreneurs. Each interview was on a CD and I began listening to them in my car each day as I drove back and forth to school and then to my real estate appointments.

One day I was listening to a CD where a man described how he was setting up one page websites to sell eBooks and other information products on highly searched, very specific topics. People could make a purchase of this information and download it immediately. We went on to explain more of the details and by the time I had arrived at my destination I was hooked. Within a week I had done my own research and was on to my way to becoming an online entrepreneur.

As a local business owner, or someone marketing for small businesses, determine the story of the owner and/or the business at the very beginning. Think about some of the most famous stories from businesses over the years for inspiration. Envision the story as a movie, where every detail is brought to life in vivid color and rich patterns and textures.

I have been marketing for a national clothing store for more than five years now and have been a part of creating and developing the stories they are sharing with their customers and prospects. Each story is based on a true series of events from the past and then modified and updated for current times. Some of the stories are deeply touching and poignant, while others are funny or hard hitting in reality. No matter which story this company decides to use in their marketing and advertising it is always one that makes an impression on the person reading the copy or viewing the commercials. This makes them a company known for going deep instead of joining the fray of shallow ideas and concepts.

My "after" story includes details of how I went from struggling with writing and technology and finally figured out how to bring it all together so that I could earn some money online. During that first year and a half I had replaced my previous income from real estate and teaching and was excited to continue learning and growing as my income increased.

My second "after" the story of what happened next and how I am continuing to be successful in my new life as an author and entrepreneur. This entails my journey to authorship, where my first book, Huge Profits with a Tiny List: 50 Ways to Use Relationship Marketing to Increase Your Bottom Line, began as a list of ten tips, was expanded to twenty-five tips and blog posts, and then compiled and reworked to become a full length book. I also share how this led to speaking engagements around the world, my first mentor program, and finally increasing my income to ten times as much as I earned while working as a classroom teacher and real estate broker/residential appraiser.

Make your stories come alive as they might in a movie. Who can ever forget Elliot and his friends taking ET to the clearing in the woods so that he could connect with the spaceship and return home? ET's head was covered with Elliot's favorite hoodie to protect him from the wind as he sat in the basket on the front of Elliot's bike. When the time was running short and the adults closed in on them all of the bicycle's were lifted off the ground so they could evade the authorities and get to the meeting place safely. can you hear the theme music as you read this?

And when Andy Dufresne, Tim Robbins' character in the film The Shawshank Redemption arrives at the prison on the bus the first day we know he is in for a difficult adjustment. The narrator tells his "before" story of being a banker in his previous life. There are flashbacks to show us how he dressed and handled himself. Then we see his wife with her lover and understand even more about this character. When the wife and her lover are murdered in bed at a country club in the next town over from his, he is the most logical suspect. But we are also told by the narrator and shown through the images that the murder was actually committed by an ex-convict who took advantage of the circumstances and made his move in order to rob the couple of their cash and other belongings on that fateful night.

When I began marketing for the handyman I shared stories of how he had built a home in his native homeland of Sweden many years ago. Then I wrote about his decision to move to the United States in 1992. Finally, I shared the details of how he was using some of these same craftsman skills as he made repairs and alterations to his client's houses in his new home country.

This served a dual purpose, as it was important to establish that he was now a United States citizen, holding dual citizenship in the U.S. as well as Sweden. There was also the perception that having a European craftsman change your faucets or clear your rain gutters was superior to having this work done by anyone else.

I wrote about all of this on the "About" page on his website, making it a simple process for every visitor to learn about his before, after, and final after stories in regards to his business, instead of asking him when they met in person or leaving it to the interpretation of his prospects and customers. If you don't share your story with others, they will come up with one of their own that will more than likely be based upon their imagination instead of the truth based on verifiable facts.

Your Story and Small Business Branding

How did you get to where you are today? The back story, which to you might seem boring and uneventful is a powerful tool that can help solidify your brand and attract just the right audience.

One of my colleagues in the online marketing space, Melissa Ingold tells of being a struggling single mother, and of creating an online business rather than simply choosing to work one dead-end job after another. Her success is an inspiration to her audience, and is a huge part of her branding.

Kelly McCausey speaks often of how she got started online when she was looking for a way to earn just a few extra dollars every month to keep the lights on. Creating graphics at five dollars each quickly turned into a full-time online career.

With a new baby at home after a cross country move, Nicole Deal opted to stay home and start a business online while her husband was at work during the day.

Gary Vaynerchuk is an example of someone whose personal brand somehow became a little bigger than life. He says:

"For those that don't know me, in my earlier days as a budding businessman and entrepreneur, I took my passion for wine and turned that into one of the biggest shows and channels on YouTube. That show landed me appearances on The Conan O'Brien Show, Ellen, CNN, etc. while amassing a social following of millions and establishing me as a "guru" (I'm not a guru) of sorts in the Social Media, Marketing, and Personal Branding worlds. From there, I became an early investor in platforms like Twitter, Tumblr, and Facebook and co-founded VaynerMedia, which is now a 600 person digital agency that represents the social presence of brands like Pepsi-Co, General Electric, and Anheuser-Busch InBev."

And my own story includes details of how I worked for twenty years as a classroom teacher while simultaneously working in real estate. After multiple bouts with cancer and a serious work injury I was ready to change my life completely and became an online entrepreneur. I struggled with the writing and the technology and pushed through to success.

Your story doesn't have to be dramatic, and you certainly don't have to share more than you're comfortable with, but it does have to be yours. Be your true self, and you will never have to worry about attracting the right audience. They will self-select, and your perfect client will find you.

Email Marketing

Yet another way to leverage the power of the internet is through email marketing. Before I explain this strategy in great detail I would like to say a little more about sending email messages to your prospects and customers.

When I started out by marketing for the handyman more than a decade ago, my own business was in its infancy and I had less than a hundred names on my list.

What I mean here when I refer to the term "list" is the database of the names and email addresses of your prospects, customers, and clients. This must be a "permission based" list of the people who have either opted in to your website or given you their express written permission to add their name and address. Also, in order to comply with the CAN-SPAM Act of 2003 they must be able to scroll to the bottom of any email message you send to them and unsubscribe with one click.

The Controlling the Assault of Non-Solicited Pornography and Marketing (CAN-SPAM) Act of 2003 was signed into law by President George W. Bush on December 16, 2003. This Act established the United States' first national standards for the sending of commercial e-mail and requires the Federal Trade Commission (FTC) to enforce its provisions.

A part of this Act is referred to as "content compliance" and requires accurate "From" lines, relevant subject lines that are not deceptive, and a legitimate physical address of the publisher and/or advertiser.

In the fine print it states that there are no restrictions against a company emailing its existing customers or anyone who has inquired about its products or services, even if these individuals have not given permission, as these messages are classified as "relationship" messages under CAN-SPAM. But when sending unsolicited commercial emails, it must be stated that the email is an advertisement or a marketing solicitation.

Even though the law makes some provisions for emailing prospects and customers without their express permission, I continue to advise my clients to have each person opt in to an email list or have them sign something to that effect before sending the first email, as I mentioned above.

With all that said and with the legalities out of the way I will tell you that email is the most effective way to reach and stay in contact with people who are interested in and could benefit from your services.

Each day in my own business as an author and entrepreneur I engage in writing such messages in order to share valuable free training and insights, make relevant offers for my products and courses, and tell stories that make a relevant point. In addition, I encourage my community to further connect with me by responding to these emails, following and friending me on social media, listening and subscribing to my podcasts, reading and commenting on my blog posts, and attending and interacting with me on my free series of teleseminars and webinars. There is no better way to let your prospects and customers know what is happening within the realm of your business and how they may get involved in a variety of ways in order to learn more and benefit in a greater way.

For example, when I market for dentists I recommend they send emails that will help people enjoy better dental health in between office visits and to become more knowledgeable about issues that are likely to arise before they occur.

Email is capable of educating your market on a mass level so that the individuals whom you can best help will pick up the phone and call your office.

The proven strategies of leveraging the power of the internet with your WordPress website, virtual storytelling, and email marketing will give you an unfair advantage and competitive edge against any competition that comes your way. You'll learn even more about using each of these to market to your business in Section Four on How to Market for Your Small Business.

Section Two – Why Is Marketing Important?

"Marketing is too important to be left to the marketing department."
~ David Packard

I have started this book with a first section that explains exactly what I mean when I use the word "marketing" in regards to local business marketing and making the phone ring. It was necessary to provide you with some historical details that would lead logically to the topics of advertising through the centuries, building strategic relationships, positioning yourself as an expert, and local networking.

Then I discussed websites, which have been around for just over two decades and how they have evolved to the point where everyone is able to set one up easily and share their message with the world. We have come a long way over these twenty-something years and now every person who can write a paragraph on the computer using a word processing program now has within them the ability and the skill to create web pages and sites of some sophistication.

Additional strategies on leveraging the power of the internet these days includes virtual storytelling and email marketing.

Why is this important for local businesses? In this Section I will discuss reaching your target market, defining your brand, becoming a household name, and exceeding your potential through your actions and efforts each day.

Focus on learning these skills which may be entirely new concepts to you and you will always be able to keep the doors to your business open as you create your own economy.

Branding

"Your brand is a story unfolding across all customer touch points."
~ Jonah Sachs

Before we talk about branding we must first have a discussion around defining, refining that definition, and finding your target audience and market. Who are these people you wish to serve, to the exclusion of nearly everyone else on the planet?

If your answer is that everyone is a potential prospect and customer that will limit your results. Seeking to serve everyone actually means you will serve almost no one. Why? Because we all prefer to have choices and to differentiate between the businesses we consider as those which will best serve our needs. Allow me to share an example of exactly what I mean by this.

When I moved to a new city I sought out a new veterinarian. I searched online and found half a dozen veterinary offices that were all somewhat similar in what they had to offer. Then I located one that stood out from the others and seemed like the perfect office for me.

This veterinarian had three other vets working in his office. He explained that he was originally from Montana and had worked with farm animals for a decade before relocating to southern California. He now considered himself to be a "large animal" vet who worked with domesticated pets. He had a photo of himself with a Great Dane on one side and an Irish wolfhound on the other.

That did not describe my needs so I kept reading. The next veterinarian working in this office was a woman. I had wanted to become a veterinarian as a younger person so this caught my attention right away. She described herself as someone who preferred to work with small and medium sized dogs and cats. That was for me! With several little dogs and two cats she could be perfect for my needs.

But it was the third veterinarian in this office that clinched the deal. This woman specialized in reptiles and some exotic animals. This was when I had Mortimer, a king snake who had previously been a class pet while I was working as a classroom teacher. She could be there for him, if and when that was needed.

There was additional information that stated they did not specialize in cats, and a recommendation was provided for a veterinarian who did. They also reiterated that even though the primary vet had prior experience with farm animals he no longer treated them. Another local recommendation was included for those who kept horses.

Over the years this veterinary office has taken care of Mortimer's respiratory infection, to which he finally succumbed a few years later, successfully delivered a litter of Morkies (these are a Maltese Yorkshire Terrier mix) by Cesarean Section, and treated a variety of illnesses and one possible broken leg that thankfully was only a serious sprain.

Now this particular veterinarian was able to broaden his reach by adding to more vets in his office, but he still does not reach out to a target audience that is out of the sphere of his experience or interest. In fact, when you call for an appointment as a new client you are questioned about your animal family members. If you only have cats you are reminded they do not specialize in cats. If you have dogs and cats and a snake, but also mention a pot-bellied pig you are reminded that the pig will be best treated by another vet, and the recommendation is provided.

What if there was no information as to the types of pets this veterinarian could adequately provide care for? Imagine making an appointment and finding out once you are there they cannot do what is needed. Instead of serving everyone, they are consciously choosing to serve fewer clients in a more specialized way.

Specialize as a way to set yourself apart and soon you will be in high demand, no matter what your business. Define the audience you wish to target and serve; refine that audience over time, based on your experience and interests, as well as the current marketplace; then locate that target audience and market to them in the ways I am sharing with you here. And always be ready to make small shifts in your target audience as the marketplace will shift over time.

Branding Your Business

I'll use ice cream to get us started. This is an excellent example of how companies and flavors drive business and sales with the benefit of excellent marketing.

What flavor ice cream do you like best? Mine used to be Jamoca Almond Fudge before I switched to Rocky Road. Why did I change over from one flavor to another, when both were available at my local Baskin-Robbins? I actually liked the ingredients of my original favorite, coffee flavored ice cream with chucks of real chocolate and toasted almonds, far more than I did Rocky Road. Dreyer's Ice Cream attempted a slight variation, called Mocha Almond Fudge but its popularity at first fluctuated and then waned over the years and I cannot remember seeing it in the store's frozen ice cream section since the turn of the century. It was the branding that made me change my behavior and affinity towards Rocky Road, plain and simple.

Rocky Road has its own Wikipedia page. It has a recipe that can be shared, with permission. It has a story. It is a "brand."

This flavor was originally created in March 1929 by William Dreyer in Oakland, California when he cut up walnuts and marshmallows with his wife's sewing scissors and added them to his chocolate ice cream in a manner that reflected how his partner Joseph Edy's chocolate candy creation incorporated walnuts and marshmallow pieces. Later, the walnuts would be replaced by pieces of toasted almond. After the Wall Street Crash of 1929, Dreyer and Edy gave the flavor its current name "to give folks something to smile about in the midst of the Great Depression." I had thought that was what Shirley Temple did for America with her singing and dancing and acting in movies that made everyone forget about the state of the economy during the 1930s. Perhaps she had a scoop of Rocky Road ice cream after lunch each day.

I predict a future with families and friends reminiscing decades from now about special occasions where Rocky Road ice cream was involved, while jamoca almond fudge will one day evaporate from our memories forever.

How can your business become the flavor fondly remembered in the hearts and minds of your target audience? They say it can take forever to build a reputation and a split second to destroy it, but in building a brand there is much more at stake.

Long gone are the days when an ad in the newspaper, a roadside billboard and a stack of colorful flyers are enough to get you noticed. These days if you don't take the time to establish your business brand online chances are you will quickly be overshadowed by your competition or even worse never get noticed by that group of people you have defined as being in your target audience and whom you wish to serve.

Branding is one of the most important aspects of any business, yet it is most often given a back seat or ignored altogether. When done right it will give you a competitive edge over others in your niche and will help you stand out in even the most competitive markets. Effective branding is all about the image of your business. Contrary to common belief it is about much more than just a fancy logo and a catchy tagline. Branding is about the perceived image of your business and what it can do for your customer. Remember WIIFM, which stands for "what's in it for me." Your prospects and customers are not being selfish with this line of thinking; they are looking out for themselves and their families with every purchasing decision they make.

Your branding tells consumers what they can expect from you, your products, and your services, and sets you apart from everyone else in the marketplace. It is derived from who you are, what you want your business to be and what people perceive it to be. Think of it like a promise you're making to your customer in advance of them making a purchase.

A good branding strategy includes multiple aspects that paint a picture of your business to consumers across multiple channels. This can include your website, social media channels, and content syndication. The goal is to make it easy for consumers to recognize your business the instant they see it no matter where they're looking. Your brand can include anything that gives your company an identity that consumers know, like and trust.

The goal is to differentiate your business from your competitors. This process must start as soon as you name your business and factor in on every decision you make from your logo and tagline to your content and advertising. You want to come up with something memorable that explains your brand promise.

For example, when M&M says their candy "Melts in your mouth, not in your hands" and Nike says, "Just Do It," we immediately know what they are all about. You can go anywhere in the world, see their logo and know exactly who they are.

No matter where your business is right now on the continuum of success, try to imagine yourself at the top and it will help you come up with creative ways to brand your business so that it is easily remembered by potential customers.

Distinction is a very important part of your brand strategy. It lets people know you have something unique to offer that's above and beyond what your competitors have. Keep in mind that your branding will impact sales and when you create a one that is easily recognized and remembered (in a good way), then you will see much better results overall.

The first step for a successful business is taking the time to let people know who you are, what you do, and how you do it. Take some time right now to think about how you want your customers to perceive your business.

Start by asking yourself these questions:

- What are your business's Mission Statement and your Vision?
- What are the benefits and features of your products or services?
- What do your customers and prospects already think of your business?
- What qualities do you want them to associate with your business?
- With any branding campaign, the goal is to spark an emotional connection between your customer and your business. When you can accomplish this, you will create a loyal following of people that cannot wait to buy what you offer.

When it comes to building a strong brand, perception is everything. This is especially true when you're trying to stand out in a competitive niche. Elon Musk tells us that "brand is just a perception, and perception will match reality over time." Being perceived as "the best" in a customer's mind can be the difference between success and failure. There are many examples of this precept through the ages. The world perceived Rocky Road to be the best ice cream flavor, or at least superior in taste to jamoca almond fudge. If you can manage tap into your customers minds and get them connect with your business on multiple touch points you will be rewarded with a loyal following of brand advocates.

YOU as the Brand

Here's an important secret successful marketers know and where small business branding comes into play: customers don't buy a product. They buy you.

Your personality. Your experience. The unique qualities only you possess.

There was a time long ago when "branding" meant a corporate-looking logo and a slick catalog, but in today's online marketplace, the real value is not in appearing to be a big company, but rather in just being you. And your personality shines through in a variety of ways.

I was at a conference recently where some of the top experts in the field of small business branding were teaching us how to effectively brand what we do online. Here are some tips they shared that you may find useful:

Your Authentic Voice

How you speak and write and even how you act on camera or in an audio interview has the power to instantly identify you to your audience. You can see this in action if you scroll through your Facebook feed. It's easy to know who has posted a particular image or status update, just by recognizing the voice with which they generally speak. This is crucial to small business branding.

Here's an even more important aspect of your "voice" though: it has the power to attract a specific audience. In recent years, a few high profile coaches and product sellers have become celebrities of a sort, largely because of their harsh, "don't hold back" language. Ash Ambirge over at The Middle Finger Project makes no apologies for her use of offensive words, and her fans love her for it. And those that do not? Well, as she says right on her home page, her site and services are "not for humorless bores." This approach is a refreshing one in a world of homogeneous conformists.

Snarkiness and foul language is not the only way to go, though. Carrie Wilkerson has built her brand almost entirely on her ability to be kind and generous. She always has a nice word, never appears defeated or overwhelmed, and is an inspiration to her fans and clients.

While very different in their approach, these two women have one thing in common: authenticity. It's clear that if you were to meet either of them in person, they would speak and act exactly as they do online. And their brands are stronger for it.

What is Your Cause?

When I work with a small business I want to know how they envision their Mission and their Vision. I define these as:

Mission - Typically a company will create a Mission Statement to share their reason for being in existence. It comes in the form of a Mission Statement and is action-oriented in declaring why you are in business and how you plan to serve those who come to you for your products and services. It defines your goals, ethics, values, and culture. The Mission Statement can become a road map for your Vision for your company.

Vision - Your Vision describes where your company aspires to be upon achieving its mission. This statement reveals the "where" of a business, but not just where your company seeks to be. Rather, a vision statement describes where the company wants a community, or the world, to be as a result of the company's services.

Write (or rewrite) your Mission Statement using this template:

- Define your purpose for being in business. Start with a story that defines your market. Imagine a real person making the actual decision to buy what you sell. Use your imagination to see why she wants it, how she finds you, and what buying from you does for her. The more concrete the story, the better. And keep that in mind for the actual mission statement wording: "The more concrete, the better." A really good market-defining story explains the need, or the want, or—if you like jargon—the so-called "why to buy." It defines the target customer, or "buyer persona." And it defines how your business is different from most others, or even unique. It simplifies thinking about what a business isn't, what it doesn't do.
- Define what your business will do for your clients in specific terms. Start with the good work you do.
- Inspire us with your dreams and goals. Patagonia aspires to "build the best product, cause no unnecessary harm, use business to inspire and implement solutions to the environmental crisis." Wow. If they are doing this even half of the time I am impressed and want to know more. I am a long time customer and raving fan of this company that is

43

headquartered less than an hour from both of the cities I call home. They were originally founded in 1973 by Yvon Chouinard, and accomplished rock climber.

- Edit, review, and revise to make every word count and to avoid wordiness. Succinctness is the key to a Mission Statement. Chipotle's is "food with integrity."

Your Vision is something that will morph over time. It can serve as a foundation to a strategic plan of broader range in the future. As I stated above, your Vision describes where your company aspires to be upon achieving its Mission and where you wish the world (or your community) to be as a result of the services you offer.

This is what LinkedIn shares with the world:

Mission

The mission of LinkedIn is simple: connect the world's professionals to make them more productive and successful. And their Vision is just as powerful with it simple and straightforward message.

Vision

Create economic opportunity for every member of the global workforce.

Who Are We?

LinkedIn began in co-founder Reid Hoffman's living room in 2002 and was officially launched on May 5, 2003.

I like how they added the "Who Are We?" section, and I will begin doing this as well for myself and my local business clients.

After I have discussed both the Mission Statement and the Vision at length with the business owner I next want to know which charitable cause they identify with and participate in on a regular basis. Over the past decade I have been involved in local business marketing this has become a more familiar and accepted concept, but it was a foreign one to the majority of small businesses before the turn of the century.

Are you familiar with the "Newman's Own" brand? It was created by the late actor Paul Newman, along with a friend, editor, novelist, playwright, and biographer Aaron Edward Hotchner in 1982. The two of them started making homemade salad dressing, bottling it and giving to friends as gifts. It was so well received they decided to go commercial and sell it to the public. Newman and Hotchner each invested twenty thousand dollars and the Newman's Own line of salad dressings was born. More food items followed and the business grew by leaps and bounds, many times far ahead of the competition.

Neither of these men needed the money from this business, and the decision was made to donate one hundred percent of the after-tax profits from the sale of its products to the Newman's Own Foundation, a private non-profit foundation which in turn gives the money to various educational and charitable organizations. As of this writing in the spring of 2019 the donated profits have exceeded forty million dollars, based on gross sales approaching seven hundred million.

These results have been documented and are nothing less than miraculous in nature. Paul Newman, an A-list actor and producer was able to successfully brand himself as a philanthropist with this venture. This opened doors to greater opportunities in his career, which in turn boomeranged with higher sales of his expanded line of food items and more philanthropy.

Much of the focus for the worthy causes he donates to is around helping children and the arts.

Your cause must make sense for your business. I am involved in a number of projects to benefit children in need. This is due to my upbringing as a child of poverty and wanting to give back to children so they may have opportunities and experiences they might otherwise miss.

Exceeding Your Potential

"Continuous effort, not strength or intelligence, is the key
to unlocking our potential."
~ Winston Churchill

I have written an entire book around this topic, entitled Rethinking the Work Ethic: Embrace the Struggle and Exceed Your Own Potential and published in 2017. I believe the concepts covered within these pages are so powerful every small business owner and their team must familiarize themselves with them and implement the proven strategies on a daily basis.

Just by starting a business you have set yourself apart from others who are not confident enough to do so. During my twenty years working as a classroom teacher I only encountered about a dozen other teachers who also had a small business away from their job at school.

During my first year I was talking about my real estate business often, until another teacher took me aside and told me to be careful doing this. She explained they were uncomfortable discussing business and would be jealous and resentful to know I had the ability to run a business and earn income in this way when they believed it was something they could not achieve. She was also in real estate and had been for longer than she had been a teacher. I silently questioned her interpretation of the situation, but during that first school year her observations proved to be a valid assessment.

If only I had treated my teaching job like I did my business every single day during those two decades. When it came to my real estate business I was willing to do whatever it took in order to succeed. I went over and above with each transaction and in every way. In my dealings with the other teachers and the administration I was easily intimidated and backed down to bullies at the first sign of confrontation. The result was mostly mediocre work on my part day in and day out, interspersed with short spurts of excellence and a high work ethic.

As a business owner I want you to elevate your status in your mind and through your actions. You are someone who helps to keep the economy going, employs others to maintain a high level of employment in your community (and perhaps beyond), and are a trusted role model for both the people who work for you as well as for others in the community.

The decisions and choices you may can have a far reaching effect and you will be looked up to by those who wish to emulate your success. As a child it was the business owners who had the greatest impact in my life. The couple who owned the local market took time to talk with me regularly. They wanted to know what I was learning in school and what I wanted to do when I grew up. And when I won the Spelling Bee in fifth grade they were more excited than I was and presented me with a handwritten card and a twenty dollar bill tucked into the envelope the following day.

Business owners are leaders. Due to the nature of any business they have become problem solvers and strategizers and negotiators and creative thinkers. Instead of being satisfied working for others for a paycheck they must make something happen so the business can remain solvent and prosperous. Be proud of what you have achieved and the direction you have chosen to take your life.

Good. Better. Best.

Being good at something is not enough. Good is fine and adequate but not how you want to be thought of in your business. If a restaurant serves good food they are likely to be out of business within their first year. Retailers selling good clothing will find themselves having to mark down prices and hold weekly sales to stay in business. Mervyn's is no longer around for this very reason.

I was always a good teacher but only made a name for myself and elevated my status when I became better and finally the best at my school in specific areas of specialization, and in my case this was science and technology.

You must work to exceed your potential in your business every single day. Begin in one area and then expand to others. I chose customer service and made it a focus and goal to exceed my potential and to surpass the service given to customers when they purchased digital products from me.

The first thing I did was to make a study of what was already being offered by others in my industry. What was the procedure when someone had a question or an issue with a product they purchased, especially when it was three in the morning for the entrepreneur who was selling the product? The results varied and ran the gamut from being totally unacceptable to being very good.

Here was what I came up with during my research period:

- Some customers were asked to submit a ticket to a help desk and told they would hear back within two business days, excluding weekends and holidays. This meant that if you had an issue on a Friday evening it could be Tuesday before you heard back, or Wednesday if that Monday were a holiday. Unacceptable.
- You were asked to submit a ticket and twenty-four hour service was promised. Good.
- You were told to hit "reply" to any email from the entrepreneur and that they would get back to you as soon as possible. For those who answered my email within twelve hours or less, I give them a Very Good rating.

My goal was to become known for speedy customer service and prompt reconciliation of any issues. I have two virtual assistants, one of whom lives on the other side of the world from me who help monitor my email accounts. When someone needs assistance with a lost password, download that does not work the first or second time, or with any other issue or technical problem or even just a question one of the three of us will typically answer within four hours. There are exceptions, of course but the overall goal is timely service with a virtual smile and we are able to easily accomplish this. By putting myself into the shoes of my customer I was able to determine what the best customer service solution would be and to find a way to deliver that solution easily.

You are a leader, within your business as well as in your community. Leadership begets success and is worth your time and effort to pursue and improve upon. My belief is that there are some born leaders and many leaders who worked to embrace these traits and characteristics over time.

One way to develop the habits and actions of a leader is through volunteering. I have already shared how I became active in my local Rotary Club soon after coming online. Almost immediately I was thrust into a position of leadership when I volunteered with the members on projects in the community. When there is work to be accomplished and you are ready to step up that's when you can feel that you are moving into a position of leadership.

Most recently I was helping at the annual Cowboy Festival, where Rotary prepares homemade peach cobbler and pulled pork sandwiches to sell to those who are attending the festival over the weekend. Within an hour of my arrival I was thrust into leadership as I organized several new volunteers and got us all into action in a logical way. Even though I was surrounded by more experienced people I was given that opportunity to practice my communication skills and make everything happen in a timely manner.

You learn the most when something goes wrong or not as planned. In this case our main organizer for this event was seriously injured six weeks before the event and was only able to participate on a limited basis. This gave all of us the opportunity to step up and take over tasks and activities that we may not have been familiar with but were a required part of this fundraising for the Club. It was on the job experience for many of us and we all pulled together to make this a successful weekend and one where we all became closer friends as a result. We performed well as a team, learned new skills, and didn't miss a beat in setting everything up and serving the customers delicious food items. And best of all we raised more money than in any previous year, which will all go to funding the projects of many other non-profits in the community.

I will remind you that I am not in any way suggesting that you or what you do must be perfect. Far from it. Instead, make your goal one in which excellence is the normal way you approach and complete all tasks and activities. Send mediocrity on its way and welcome the excellence that will turn you into the awesome version of yourself forever.

What Would "Awesome" You Do?

I had never used the word "awesome" as a regular part of my

vocabulary until I came online as an entrepreneur in 2006. Once I began working with local businesses to assist them in their marketing goals I was soon in awe of the people I encountered.

Small businesses keep the American economy moving forward, and the creativity and innovation I have seen first-hand is nothing short of miraculous in nature. What happens in the States then has the boomerang effect as far as what is possible. These achievements and what is accomplished ripple across the pond and far beyond.

During the past decade I have made it a priority to be as awesome as possible in both my personal and professional life, always asking myself the question "What would awesome Connie do?" in each situation I encounter.

Exceeding your potential as a business owner could begin with the same question. This will make you stop and think before you speak or act and will result in a more satisfying outcome.

Finding High Achieving Team Members

It is one thing to have lofty goals for your business that will exceed your potential on a regular basis. It is quite another to find others who will share your vision, at least during the hours you are employing them or they are working on tasks and activities for you as a freelancer or independent contractor.

I was not used to or familiar with the concept of hiring freelancers and independent contractors to help me with my work. But once I came online I realized immediately I did not have the technical skills to accomplish everything on my own. This led to lots of frustration as I attempted to find the right people to help me run my business. I also needed help with customer service and decided to look for someone to help me with that as well. Finally, I accepted the fact that I would need help with graphic design for my websites and other aspects of my business.

For the technology help I needed I went to someone I had met while attending a Marketing Retreat and Mastermind in Virginia during my first year as an entrepreneur. This woman was very smart and working as a freelancer for someone who had been doing what I wanted to do for many years. She needed additional clients and she and I came to a barter arrangement during my first year. She set up sites for me using HTML (this was before WordPress became the industry standard) and also created gorgeous graphics for me as well. After a year I began paying her and our business relationship lasted until she took a full time job at a local college. It never mattered that she was three time zones away on the opposite coast.

When I searched for someone to help me with customer service I decided to choose someone who lived in Santa Clarita, where I still live part of the time when I am not in Santa Barbara. She worked as the director of a local non-profit during the week and had taken a part-time job at a clothing store at the mall in order to earn some additional income and pay off some bills. That job paid minimum wage and required her to work one evening each week, as well as on Saturday and Sunday.

When we had a discussion about her coming to work for me it seemed like the perfect fit. I needed her for twelve hours each week, the same as what she was putting in at the clothing store. I would start her at more than she was earning there. Also, she could do the twelve hours of work each week on the days and times that were convenient for her instead of at specific days and times each week as required by any job where you are an hourly employee. We shook hands and she began about a week and a half later after giving notice at the clothing store.

This arrangement worked well for the first two weeks and then everything changed. When I noticed that work was not being completed I contacted her immediately.

Even though this was a smart, capable, mature person who had held jobs of responsibility during her adult life, somehow this did not translate to working as an independent contractor. She and her husband were now going out of town on the weekends and my work was not getting done. We had a couple of conversations after the initial one and then I had to let her go. Because we lived in the same city and had overlapping circles of influence and friends it was awkward for awhile. I made every effort to salvage the relationship and was successful in making this happen.

The lesson I learned from this was that I was not capable of training someone to be a virtual assistant because I had not worked with enough other people in this capacity to know how to bring them aboard and have them complete important tasks and become a part of my team. I found that hiring people who already worked for others was best. My goal was to meet people at live events, those I host and others I attend and speak at in order to get recommendations for those who were available to do what I needed. Now I have fifteen people working virtually for me. Most of them are in North America, two are in Europe and one is in Malaysia. Each person works for several people and is a high achieving team member and collaborator.

The way you handle this aspect of your business will dictate how successful you will be. My recommendation is that your bring people aboard one at a time, spend the time necessary to explain exactly what you need them to do and how you want it done. Also, assign them a mentor within your business to answer questions and to review the work so they feel like part of your company and connected with others there.

Section Three – What Can You Expect?

"The aim of marketing is to know and understand the customer so well the product or service fits him and sells itself."
~ Peter F. Drucker

If you take action on what I am sharing here and market for your small business in this new way you can expect to see noticeable results in three months, or even less time in some cases.

Even if you have been running your business for decades, and perhaps even more so if you have been at it for that long a time, it makes sense for you to learn and implement new and updated strategies that are working now.

The fact that you've read this far in the book shows that you have a genuine interest in making measurable improvements in what you are doing with your marketing, assuming you have read straight through since the beginning of the book.

I always say that marketing is the area I was meant to learn and share with others. I make it fun and continue to experience excellent results within my own business and for the plethora of other businesses I am connected with in some capacity.

You may not be as excited as I am, or cannot imagine marketing to be fun, but if you are willing to put even half of my ideas, systems, and strategies into place you will be ahead of at least more than half of the small business owners today.

Take some time to review the five chapters leading up to this section. Review your notes, if you took some and implement one new thing before the end of this week.

Perhaps you will take a fresh look at your website to see if it is set up in a way that will attract the right customers into your business. Maybe you will review your customer avatar to decide if your customer avatar needs updating. Or you may decide to work on your storytelling or branding. Whatever the case, continue to keep an open mind and embrace what I am sharing with you within these pages as information that can change your experience as a business owner in a major way.

Your Business Growth Plan

"Word of mouth can be as important, if not more important, for neighborhood businesses as traditional advertising."
~ Ekaterina Walter

Now it's time to navigate past the basics of local business marketing and move full-fledged into the world of sales, revenue, and marketing. Believe that you are a pillar of the community and keep the economy running smoothly by prospering as a business owner. By adopting this belief as your mantra you are able to change lives and help to create a stronger connection with people from every area in your community. This could encompass education, technology, medicine, industry, and more. It's a powerful way to accept responsibility that will lead to a greater future for our children.

What Do I Mean By "the Basics"?

The basics of business include opening your doors and remaining solvent. These include taking up space in a building that suits your needs, at least for the time being; hiring the people who will allow you to serve others; and bringing in enough revenue to make your business what is known as a "going concern." The definition of this phrase is a business that functions without the threat of liquidation for the foreseeable future, which is usually regarded as at least the next twelve months. "Going concern" implies for the business the basic declaration of intention to keep operating its activities at least for the next year. This takes a personal and financial commitment but is still basic in nature.

Being willing to accept the challenge of going beyond these basics makes it possible for you to build and grow a business that will continue on for generations, perhaps within your own family and leave a legacy to those who will lead our world in the future. I had the pleasure of working with a legacy insurance company that was being run by the third generation, while training the fourth generation to take over when they completed their formal education. We discussed how the foundation had been laid at the turn of the twentieth century and how that enabled them to move past the basics as they entered the twenty-first century.

A powerful way for you to do this with your own company, no matter how long you have been in business is to develop strong relationships with other business owners in your city and beyond. I've discussed the idea of joining your local Chamber of Commerce and also a service organization. I used Rotary as an example of such an organization.

Several years ago I was a marketing consultant for a family who owned several movie theatres. It was an interesting story that included two brothers making the decision to stay at their jobs until they could get their business up and running. They each purchased a movie theatre in their community, and these cities were about two hours apart in the Pacific Northwest. This was during the 1960s when the local movie theatre was the center of entertainment and socialization in any small city (less than fifty thousand inhabitants) and before cable television or VHS tapes were available.

Their target audiences were almost identical, as well as their demographics and population size. Over the years they experimented with different types of sales and marketing strategies. Sometimes they did the same exact thing to see if their results varied. Other times they tested out an idea independently and then shared the results with each other afterward.

It wasn't until they each joined their respective service organizations almost a decade later, one choosing Rotary and the other joining the Kiwanis Club that they experienced the success they had been hoping for all along. Then they were able to quit their jobs and become full time business owners.

The reason for this is two-fold. One, they now had a small army of business owners to run ideas by and to mastermind with on a regular basis. Even though none of them had ever owned a movie theatre they had decades of experience running businesses. Two, they now had access to every other business, non-profit, and governmental entity in each of their respective communities as team members with whom they could partner.

The school district wanted to discuss family nights, awards for the students, and fundraisers that would benefit the theatres as well as the students and their families. A shoe store pitched an idea for collecting shoes for people in need in return for movie tickets for those who purchased shoes at their store. A restaurant offered a twenty percent discount on food items in exchange for a spot in the monthly newsletter that was mailed out to regular patrons and also available at the theatre. Remember, this was all long before the internet and even before personal computers and mobile phones, if you can remember back that far.

I learned so much from consulting with this family, now ready to enter their third generation of legacy entrepreneurship. Once they informed me that they made twelve times as much revenue from their concession stands as they did with movie tickets I had many ideas they implemented quickly to increase their bottom line.

This is also an excellent example of the concept of becoming "a resource before you're a vendor." What I mean specifically by this is to offer to be of service to others from day one so that the idea of them doing business with you becomes a no-brainer.

Here are some examples of what this can look like for small businesses.

- A hair stylist I worked with complained that she wasn't getting any new clients even though she was running a quarter page advertisement in a local magazine. When I looked at her ad I saw it was all about her and nothing specifically for her prospects. We changed it so that she was offering a free consultation for color and haircuts. Every person who came in from that ad booked a color and/or cut with her while they were sitting in her chair.
- A car mechanic I worked with had a business slump after two new auto shops opened up within a mile of his location. We wrote a blog post about the five things to pay attention to with your car or truck to extend its life for three years. It included an offer for the reader to make an appointment at no cost to check out all five items on the list. Over fifty percent of those

who made the appointment and came in had service done within the next thirty days.

- The plumbers I worked with wanted to expand beyond the Los Angeles area to a city with an oversupply of plumbing contractors. We created a seven day offer as an experiment that included a free toilet seat with every new customer call to check out their kitchen and bathrooms at no charge. A third of those visits turned into paid work that day, and another third made an appointment within the next ninety days.

In each case the prospects were surprised to receive something of value at no cost and reciprocated by paying for work to be done. Those who did not need any work done at that time referred the plumbers to friends, neighbors, and family members. The in person nature of these offers built the "know, like, and trust" factor immediately and led to additional business for the company. Reread these examples to make sure you understand how each one was positioned and how you could do something similar in your own business.

Your Business Growth Plan

This is a process of nine steps, some of which I have already covered and some that I will lay out in coming chapters.

1) Business Mission and Vision: I've discussed this is several places within this book, but it bears repeating because this is truly the starting point for any business. Without a Mission Statement and a Vision you could find yourself floundering in a sea of partially fleshed out ideas, actions, and results. Taking the time to mindfully create each of these will give you the clarity to pass on to your employees, colleagues, team members, and customers.

2) Ideal Client: This is the avatar you create for the person whom you most desire to serve. I do this on a regular basis for my own online marketing business and have helped many local business owners to create their own customer avatar. Here is my most recent one:

Lauren Shepherd is 58 years old, divorced for sixteen years, and mother to Roger, 19 and Carrie, 23, who both live at home while going to college and working part-time. Lauren graduated from California State Long Beach with a degree in economics and finance and has worked at a private corporation in Newport Beach for the past eighteen years as a senior accountant.

She drives a three year old Chevrolet Impala that currently needs to be washed. Even though it's a longer drive with more traffic she often uses the coastal route to drive to and from work, looking out at the ocean and longing to spend more time closer to the beach.

Once a month she and some friends from work spend their Friday evening in Newport Beach, having dinner at a favorite spot along the water and watching the beach goers and boaters go by. Although she doesn't have much in common with any of them and feels like some of them drink way too much, she does enjoy this time as an escape from her regular life. She thinks about moving here permanently but feels like her life is just too complicated to do that, at least until her children move out on their own.

Lauren reads books on business, especially ones on startups and online businesses. She also likes to read fantasy and novels by John Grisham and Scott Pratt. Years ago she had thought about going to law school but somehow this did not transpire. She stopped using Facebook and other social media after it became too political during the last presidential election and she only watches television occasionally when she records The Voice or other musical and awards shows she enjoys.

She dreams about starting a business and moving into a beachfront condominium in Newport Beach. She would also like to leave her job within a year and have the time and money to live very differently than she does right now. She is kept awake at night by the thought of living the way she does now until she can retire in eight years.

This is not the life she wanted to live. She is afraid of losing her independence as she grows older, as her eighty-five year old mother has in recent years. Her mother no longer drives and is now living in an assisted living community in a section of Long Beach that isn't very clean or safe.

She has two long-time friends she trusts and goes to for advice occasionally. One is a friend from college who is now dean of a private law school in L.A. The other is a man she met while she was going through her divorce. They dated a couple of times before deciding to remain friends.

Lauren always thought she would spend more time helping others, by volunteering and fund raising for non-profits. She would consider this to be doing the important work in life - helping people reach their full potential in work and activities that are meaningful to them.

To keep her mind off her worries about retirement and her future she has begun to buy products, courses, and books related to online entrepreneurship. If she could only find someone she likes and trusts she would join their coaching or mentoring program and follow their guidance and suggestions to the letter. She is still looking for that one person.

3) Business Goals - You have already addressed your "Why" with the first step, creating your Mission Statement and Vision for your business. Go deeper here, asking yourself what you wish to achieve in the next twelve months and in the next three years. I find that going past the three year mark in this exercise is not a valuable use of your time. Be specific about what you want to achieve. For example, how many new customers you want to gain and the anticipated size of your customer base at the end of the period. Try to plan some quick actions you can take for immediate gains (such as a simple addition to an existing product or service that you can offer without much additional work), as well as longer-term goals (such as developing an entirely new product line or a series of related services from scratch).

4) Marketing Tactics - Review your most current marketing assessment and make decisions on where you'll make changes in your marketing tactics. Include changes you will make to existing tactics, new tactics you will add, costs involved, and how everything will impact your goals. Impact could be things like a specific increase in revenue or decrease in cost or time. Notice here that I am discussing tactics and not strategies. Within the scope of what I am sharing with you here in these nine steps, this is the appropriate place for you to be.

5) Team Members - Do precise budgeting to decide on the right level of people resourcing for your business. It's important that resources are prioritized, so that areas of a business which are key to delivering your overall aims and objectives are adequately funded. If funding isn't available, this may involve making cutbacks in other areas. Allocate resources to reflect your business's position and future direction.

See where you can make better use of the people resources you have now, as well as where it makes sense to add new team members. Determine if they will be employees, freelancers, independent contractors, or a combination of these positions. Lay out those responsibilities, along with the costs associated with current and new team members so that you can see what additional funding you need to tap into.

Depending on the changes you make, note any cost savings too.

6) Processes and Tools - In this day and age much of what we do within the day to day activities of our business is automated, cloud based, and/or specifically related to and dependent upon software, programs, and online tools, as well as with physical tools and applications. Review these regularly to see where you need to make changes and updates to keep your business competitive and cutting edge.

7) Financial Forecast - A detailed cash flow forecast is essential for this process. This includes current revenue and expenditure as well as projected revenue and expenditure for the modifications you want to make. Enough money must be in the pot to keep the core business running, as you need to ensure that your income continues over the growth period. Your outgoings will rise sooner and faster than your revenues. Build in some surplus to your projections in case projects run over – things often take longer than you think they will.

8) Key Metrics - Determine what numbers you will look at to measure how your business is really do at any point in time. if you are not familiar with Google Analytics, learn as much as you can or bring in a team member to handle this on your behalf.

9) Milestones and Deadlines - We must set deadlines for the milestones we wish to achieve. These cannot be arbitrary numbers and dates. For example, my goal is to write and publish one full length - thirty thousand words minimum - book each calendar year, as well as one smaller one that may not even be related to my primary topic of entrepreneurship or my core business.

Incorporating Marketing into Your Life

"Humans are not ideally set up to understand logic; they are ideally set up to understand stories."
~ Roger C. Schank

The greatest compliment I can ever hear is "I see you everywhere!" For me this means I am doing my job to get the word out about who I am, what I do, and how I may serve those who are in my target market. Small business owners must do the same thing if they are to get noticed in a bigger way.

Think once again to the exact people you wish to serve. And this cannot be everyone, as I discussed earlier. Even if you are a plumber you cannot serve everyone with indoor plumbing. Instead, narrow you marketing focus to a smaller group, such as commercial buildings or homes within a specific geographical area or size of the improvements of the property. Even though you will be available to serve everyone, it makes more sense to limit your marketing to a select group in order to make a name for yourself as a specialist rather than a generalist.

If you are a consultant you could help everyone, but isn't it better to be known for serving a group that elevates your status while you are in the process of building your business?

The idea here is to incorporate marketing into your daily life. I think of it as a game that enhances my ability to reach more people and increase my income. I also learn a great deal in the process as I hone my skills and sharpen the tools in my tool box. And, finally I am able to help the people I encounter by sharing my marketing skills with those who will most benefit by implementing even something small and seemingly insignificant into their daily business.

No matter where I am and who I'm with I think about how to improve the marketing for the business I am in front of. On a recent trip to Solvang, a Danish-American community about an hour north of Santa Barbara I drove past the emu and ostrich farm located on the main road into town. They have about fifty of these graceful animals on a thirty acre spread along the Santa Ynez River.

One issue they continue to have is people pulling off the main highway in an attempt to take a picture of these creatures without having to pay the five dollar admission fee to go inside. It is not only dangerous to do this but also next to impossible to take a decent photo. Fifty animals on thirty acres means that each one will appear as a tiny speck in your photo and you will have missed out on the experience of being up close to these graceful creatures.

My solution would be to erect a large sign that tells the passersby exactly how much it will cost and what they will discover once inside. Keeping everything a mystery is costing them money and depriving many visitors to the area the opportunity to get involved.

Perhaps they could charge five dollars admission for one person, eight dollars for two, and ten dollars for up to five people in a group. Why discount the admission fee? Because their real profits come once someone is inside the gate!

There are multiple opportunities for visitors to spend money, and many more possibilities this business has not yet explored.

If I lived closer to this community I would go after this as a marketing opportunity to hone my skills with a unique niche business. I would write a blog post about them and include some observations and an idea. Next, I would pitch this article to a local publication to get the word out that I was interested in increasing their revenue. Then I would call them and make an appointment to meet with them in person to share my ideas. I did something similar with the zoo in Santa Barbara and they implemented one of my ideas into their "giraffe marketing" I had written about.

Your goal must be one of "pull" rather than "push" marketing. What I mean by this is that you want your prospects to call you more often than you have to go after them. Allow me to define and further explain each of these terms, at least in the way I perceive them.

Push marketing puts you as the marketer in complete control of the timing, and frequency of promotions. When I send out an email message to my list I am pushing my content and offers out to them. Push marketing is also referred to as outbound marketing. The hope is that the readers will develop an interest in what I am sharing and respond by making a purchase.

Pull marketing, on the other hand is all about making your products and services visible in plain sight to prospects. They can find you when they realize they have an interest in your topic and will come to you looking for answers to their questions and solutions to their problems. It consists of newer marketing channels like your blog or website, search engine optimization (SEO) applied to everything you share online and social media marketing. This is also referred to an inbound marketing.

The truth is that pull marketing is becoming more and more effective and your prospects now know where to look for you online. My YouTube channel, social media profiles, articles published on sites like Medium and LinkedIn articles, my books on Amazon, my podcast, and my two blogs are how most of my customers and clients have found me in recent times. I recommend using a combination of about 70% pull marketing and 39% push marketing. Test and course correct as necessary for your market.

I often say that if I had paid more attention to learning about marketing I would have had a very different real estate business in the years since I was first licensed in 1983. What we think about expands. What we spend time in doing each day becomes a part of our DNA. If I had thought about building my real estate business from the very first day it would have grown to the exact size I had desired.

If I had taken the time to learn everything I could about marketing and implemented everything I learned my business would have been a contender in my little corner of the world. Instead, I worked mostly by myself for more than twenty years and I was not considered to be an expert in my field. It wasn't until I began working with a mentor in 2005 that he explained how I could set up and run this business with a different mindset and goal.

I have few regrets as I believe life unfolds in the way it is meant to be. But if you have the desired goal of doing more with your business, incorporate marketing into your daily life and you will soar to new heights.

Section Four – How Do You Market for Your Small Business?

"The best marketing strategy ever: CARE."
~ Gary Vaynerchuk

The Eight-Pronged Approach to
Local Business Marketing

I will now outline the eight-pronged approach I have used successfully in my own business, as well as with dozens of small businesses all over the world. I have already shared much of these strategies in the chapters leading up to this point. This is a logical progression of how to go from where you might be right now to closer to where you would like to be as soon as possible. If your journey takes a slightly different path it simply means you are being more unique than the average small business owner.

These are the eight prongs in this marketing approach:

- Identify, Define, and Refine Your Mission and Vision for your business
- Your Website - Set up on the hosted WordPress platform, this is where the majority of your prospects will get their first

impression of you and what your company has to offer
- Content Creation, Publication, and Syndication - Content is King on the internet. This piece will involve blogging, articles, audios, videos, and slide presentations.
- Community Involvement -
- Your "Cause"
- Unique USP and Brand
- Email Marketing
- Teaching Your Topic

It all begins with your Mission and Vision for your business. I went into some detail about this in Chapter 4, where the focus was on branding your business. Take the time now, if you haven't already to refine your Mission Statement and your Vision for your business.

Once you have done this, make sure everyone on your team understands what this means and has heard you talk about it. This includes your family members, employees, freelancers, outsourcers, customers, clients, and prospects. Once someone is on board with your Mission and Vision they become a part of your community and will support you and your products and services for years to come.

When you make changes in how you do business, when the economy shifts, and when there is a situation you have little or no control over, those who understand your long term vision will be there for you.

Next comes your website. Whether or not you have a brick and mortar business or do business exclusively online your website is the first "touch" you have with your prospect. Just say someone has Googled for what they need and found you on Google Places, something you can easily set up at no cost through Google Business.

Now we move on to content creation and syndication. I touched upon this topic briefly in Chapter 3 when I discussed virtual storytelling as a way to leverage the power of the internet. The most effective way to tell stories and create relevant content is through blogging consistently. This blog will be a part of your business website and will be set up using the WordPress platform I wrote about in great detail at the beginning of the third chapter. This keeps everything simple, which has become my motto over the past decade.

I first heard about blogs (this is short for web logs) while I was still a classroom teacher. The year was 2004 and little did I know that would lead to a seven figure a year business where I would maintain two blogs and use these to build credibility, increase visibility, and grow profitably every single day.

When blogging for your business, start by writing what you know. By this I mean to share your thoughts with your readers so they can better know you and think of you as someone they know, like, and trust. Blog about your Mission and Vision for your company. Share stories that are related to what you have to offer. Encourage readers to leave a comment and to join your permission based list, whether or not they are ready to call you to discuss their situation or to make an appointment.

I marketed for an HVAC (heating, ventilation, and air conditioning) company and showed them how to do this quickly and effectively. One of their most popular posts was on the topic of what to do when your air conditioning won't turn on. What they came up with was detailed and accurate but it wasn't exactly keeping readers on the edge of their chairs to find out what happened next. So I suggested they have an infographic created to add as an image for that post. It was simple, easy to read, and colorful. It outlined the five steps to take when troubleshooting this problem.

They included checking your:

- thermostat
- air filter
- circuit breakers
- AC drain pan
- AC shutoff switch

This simplicity worked like magic to give people some basic knowledge to see if they could solve the problem on their own. Once they had gone through these five steps and their air conditioning would still not turn on it made sense to pick up the phone and call the company for an appointment. Another post address how to find out if your heater is energy efficient and the three step process to find this out.

Remember that for each post you write you will describe a common problem, give the reader some tools with which to come to a conclusion, and then present your company as the solution to this problem.

Take the mystery out of what you do, present it in a logical and concise manner and you will transform new prospects into devoted fans. A blog makes this a simple process. This works for any trade or profession as businesses are only in business to solve specific problems. A grocery store serves hungry people, a dentist serves people who have a dental issue or those who wish to prevent these issues from popping up prematurely or unnecessarily, and an HVAC company serves people who wish to heat or cool their home or business.

You may also wish to combine your blog posts and articles into short reports or "white papers" to show your prospects and customers that you are an expert in your field or industry.

Content creation also includes video, audio, and presentations. Create your own Channel on YouTube; host teleseminars and podcasts and be a guest on others, and use a simple slide presentation to share as a video and to upload to slide sharing sites.

Business is simple, so keep it simple.

I will say a few words about keywords here so that you may incorporate SEO (search engine optimization) into everything you write for your business.

Think about someone who has recently moved to Miami, Florida who would like to order a pizza to be delivered to their door. They will take out their phone or go to Google on their computer and type in something like "great pizza in Miami."

When I do this I am taken to a page with businesses listed as a part of Google business, but if I'm new in town I need to know a little bit more. The first post is an article about "The Ten Best Pizzas in Miami" and it hits the spots with detailed information, full color photos that make my mouth water and comments from happy customers sharing exactly what they like and dislike about that particular pizza. In this case the pizza is elevated to almost celebrity status and readers will have inside information to make them feel at home with their choice.

Make a list of the words and phrases someone might use to search for and describe the problem they are looking to solve. Make this an ongoing project and don't stop until you get to one hundred words and phrases. As you come up with new ones you will write a blog post using that as part of the title. Then when someone goes to Google to solve their problem you have a good chance of coming up in the results, also known as the SERPs - search engine results pages.

Community involvement is next and this one was new to me when I started my business in 2006. I simply did not understand or appreciate the power of connecting with others in the city I had just moved to, Santa Clarita, California. Once I got out and met people my business took off, even though my business was online and not based on serving people in person.

When you have a brick and mortar business you will create a strategic plan for how you will interact and participate in your local community. I would begin with your Chamber of Commerce and decide if joining is the right decision for you. Then visit a local service organization such as Rotary, Kiwanis, or Lion's to see what they are all about. You do not need to join right away, as you are still in the "research and experimentation" phase of this powerful strategy.

While you are spending time at the Chamber and with one or more of the service organizations in your city find out what projects and activities they currently are involved in that are happening soon. Show up at each of these to get a feel for what is happening and who the key people are within each group. Typically, twenty percent of the people do eighty percent of the work in any group setting, and volunteering is no different.

Imagine yourself as a member of the group. Does it feel like the proper fit? Observe the people volunteering - are these the people you wish to associate with regularly? Google the group and see what else you can find out. One of my local business clients joined an organization in his town, only to find out months later two of the members were involved in a fraudulent activity for which they were later arrested, charged, and convicted!

Now think about your "cause." This is something that makes sense for you and your business and not a random charity or non-profit organization. I have shared earlier how I grew up in poverty and any group that helps children is of interest to me. I was also a classroom teacher for twenty years before starting my marketing business so there is that connection as well.

Take your time with this and discuss it with your family and business associates. If you are in a Mastermind bring this up as a topic for discussion and idea sharing. One of my clients was sure she had no connection to any cause until a family member reminded her that their cousin had been in a motorcycle accident a few years earlier and was now a quadriplegic. The result was a connection with the Triumph Foundation, a local group whose Mission is to help children, adults, and Veterans with spinal cord injury/disorder to triumph over their disability and to inspire them to keep moving forward with their lives by pushing themselves to get better every day. My client is now very involved with this organization and this has helped her to reconnect with her cousin and to assist many people she may not have ever taken the time to meet.

Now let's dig deeper into your business and your USP. This stands for your "unique selling proposition" and is what sets you apart from the plethora of businesses that appear to be doing almost exactly what you are doing and offering the same products and/or services to people who do not know and understand how you are different. Plain vanilla might be right for an ice cream flavor but will not serve you well as a business.

This was an area I struggled with personally during my first couple of years in business. I kept saying my USP was that I cared about my clients in a way that others did not, but that was just scratching the surface of how I was different from everyone else.

My background includes twenty years of classroom teaching. During this period I was required to create detailed lesson plans around what I would be teaching my students every day. These lessons were based on the curriculum designed by professional educators across the United States and agreed upon by my employer, the Los Angeles Unified School District.

It made sense for me to do something similar as I taught my adult students how to become profitable as online entrepreneurs. They remarked about how simple it was to follow my writing and my teaching within the online courses I was teaching and my Mentor program. I was following the 7 Step Lesson Plan outline I had used for twenty years so it did not seem so special to me. This seven step outline was originally created by Dr. Madeline Hunter, a renowned educator at UCLA whose ideas and methods came into vogue during the 1960s and 1970s in public school education. Once I realized that others working online were not even familiar with lesson plans I began to get a sense of my own USP - unique selling proposition.

What sets you apart from others in your field? Make a list of what you do and how you do it each day.

Sometimes it is effective to simply point out what you do in your business, even if your competitors are doing the same or something similar in theirs. For example, if I point out that the plumbers I am marketing for are using a specific camera to view the pipes deep below the service, this doesn't say anything about the camera other plumbing companies are using. And a well known beer company grabbed a huge market share during the 1960s simply by describing their brewing process in a television commercial. The competition complained that it was unfair because everyone brewed beer in a similar way. While this was true, it only took one company to be first in using this to be seen as unique for them to excel. This isn't tricky or deceitful in any way; this is how to spotlight something you do that is cutting edge or extremely effective in solving problems for your customers.

Email marketing is next. It amazes me that more small businesses have not embraced this strategy to stay connected with their prospects and customers. This is one of the least expensive and most effective methods of marketing. When I began marketing for local businesses this was met with resistance by the owners. My goal was to uncover the reasons why they did not want to do this and to overcome the objections with logic and an open mind. The primary objection was that they believed they would be bothering people by showing up in their email inbox when this was not yet an accepted practice.

I began with a dentist I was working with and he finally agreed to try it for three months and to only send one email message each month. He had not been collecting email addresses from his patients so I commissioned a young (she was twelve years old) artist in the community to paint a picture that would be appealing and soothing to someone who had just got out of the dentist's chair. She painted a colorful fish swimming in the ocean and it was perfect. We duplicated her original art in postcard size and left a small stack on the counter. As the patient was checking out they were asked to add their email address to the list, told they would only be contacted once a month with information and perhaps a special offer, and given the postcard with the colorful fish on one side and details of how to leave a review online on the other side.

This gave the patient the choice of whether or not to be added to the email list. Permission based is the law and I discussed this in more detail in Chapter Three. The front desk people reported that only about one percent of their patients said no to this. And everyone loved receiving the colorful postcard, with about seventy percent leaving a review within the following two weeks.

The first email message welcomed them to the dentist's online community and shared some common sense information for keeping their smile a healthy and bright one. There was also an offer to pay for a third cleaning each year (insurance typically pays for two cleanings each year, but many people benefit greatly from having a third one done), as well as an invitation to invite a friend, neighbor, or family member to become a patient. It is against a law to offer a financial incentive of any kind for a referral, so I positioned it as beneficial to others to enjoy the same type of dental care they were experiencing.

Expanding your reach by teaching is the final step in my eight-pronged approach. Teaching is profitable in many ways. Home Depot continues to teach classes, some that are specific to men, women, children, and families on a variety of topics that include interior painting and drywall repair, pool care, installing tile flooring, building pegboard shelving, and more. These classes are free and then it makes sense for you to purchase the materials from them afterward.

A local candy store in my community offers classes in making your own chocolates, cake decorating, and cupcake construction. One of the non-profits I am a part of, Zonta, had them come to our location to teach us to make candy. This was a successful fundraiser that made sense for women in business dedicated to the advancement of women worldwide (Zonta's Mission Statement).

The dentist I worked with teaches within the email messages that are sent out each month. One popular topic was the effect of lemons on your tooth enamel. Many people enjoy adding fresh squeezed lemon to water in the morning, but there are important tips to follow so you do not damage your teeth in the process. This type of preventative dental care, in combination with more common sense facts about brushing after eating candy are very helpful. Even the proper methods of brushing and flossing are appreciated and can lead to clients who are more informed and aware. These are the people who will come in to the dental office more often, be thrilled to receive email messages, leave excellent online reviews, and refer others to the dentist.

One printer I know from my Rotary Club taught his customers how to upload PDF files to his site so he could have their print orders ready when they came in a few hours later. This saved them an additional trip to his store and saved him time by not having to serve them in person twice.

The ideas are endless and all lead to a heightened awareness and relationships with the people you serve.

What can you teach your prospects, customers, and clients?

Attracting the Right Clients

"I've learned that people will forget what you said, people will forget what you did, but people will never forget how you made them feel."
~ Maya Angelou

All prospects, customers and clients are not created equal. Yes, many people who connect with you will have things in common. They may even join your email list, interact with you on social media, and perhaps make a purchase or two with you over time. But they are not the right clients for you to grow your small business to the next level from where you are right now.

In Chapter 4 I discussed narrowing down your target audience. In Chapter 6 I shared my avatar when I am looking for my ideal client. But the big question remains...How do you attract the right clients for you into your business?

The Client Attraction Formula

The goal is to identify, locate, and bring into the fold the prospects, customers, and clients that are the perfect fit for you. Where are they right now and how will you be able persuade them to do business with you?

Allow me to share an example with you. This is a Case Study of the handyman I have referred to throughout this book.

I was new to local business marketing when I offered to help Claes in 2006. At this time I was also new to the community and finding my way as a new entrepreneur. When the daily newspaper advertisement and the magazine articles did not pan out as expected I was forced to dig deeper until I could make his phone ring almost effortlessly.

Necessity is indeed the mother of invention. While at lunch with my Rotary Club meeting on a Wednesday I found myself in a conversation with another Rotarian. She and her husband were headed out of town the following week for a three week trip to visit family and friends in the Midwest. She shared with me that they were still trying to find the right person to housesit for them during their time away. I inquired as to what needed to be looked after and who the right person could be. Her answer gave me a new perspective into the concept of attracting the right clients.

"We are looking for someone who is dependable, honest, and trustworthy. We have a small garden that needs tending to and two cats that are not used to being left alone. The right person would treat our home as if it were their own and make sure the animals and the plants were properly tended. There is also mail to be brought it and some other odds and ends. Above all else, we need someone we can trust."

No, I did not turn Claes into a professional house sitter, but I did have a talk with him about presenting himself to potential customers in a way that would set him apart from every other handyman in the city.

We determined that his "right" clients would be people who did not have an adult male living in the home or close by who could help them with repairs, maintenance, and replacements around their home or office. These people would also have almost unlimited disposable income, making it possible for these prospects to have this work done even if the economy was in a slump. And what they would all have in common more than anything else was the importance they gave to trustworthiness above craftsmanship. Someone possessing both of these characteristics would be a dream come true for them.

I began inviting Claes to attend fundraisers, meetings, and hands-on projects in the community. This world was new to me and it was fun to bring him along to meet my new friends and acquaintances while working on worthwhile projects.

This became my first official Case Study for local business marketing as I watched him interact with the others. He had to learn how to work the topic of his handyman business into every conversation and I was there to assist in the beginning. When someone mentioned the weather he or I would interject something about how he had adjusted for the rain or the extreme heat or the heavy winds by doing something specific on a recent or current job. If they commented on the food that was being served he would segue into a discussion of a recent job where he changed the kitchen faucet or replaced the garbage disposal so the people could more easily entertain guests on a frequent basis. Soon we included details about the pets at his customer's homes and how they took to him so easily because they could sense he loved and respected all creatures.

Within a month he could almost sense the moment someone would ask him for his business card and he was able to pull one out of his pocket in record time, without bending the corner. Later he would tell them when placing the card into their hands that he was booked for the coming week and to call him as soon as they knew what they wanted done so he could get them on his schedule as quickly as possible.

This was an evolving process of knowing what to say to whom and when to say it. Daily practice made it all come together in a profitable way. Once you make marketing fun everything shifts in your business.

The phone was ringing more than simply from the work I was doing for him with the blog and on Google with the search engine optimization (SEO) for his keyword phrases. Claes was integral to the process and his confidence grew. This also allowed him to turn down work that he didn't want to get involved in for any reason.

And if a customer was unkind or demanding or unreasonable he had no difficulty in telling them they needed to find someone else to help them. One day I overheard him speaking with a woman who was adamant about having him do some work for her that her homeowner's association did not allow. He told her he was not going to do it, thanked her for calling, and hung up the phone.

Another thing to note was that Claes was doing more volunteering in the community when the hands-on projects needed people who were handy. He worked side by side with people who had good intentions but lacked the skills to do at least some of the work. He would show them how to do the things that were needed, and in doing this was showing them he was the one to do work at their home when something needed to be repaired or replaced.

Within a few months Claes was in a power position with his handyman business. And it wasn't long before his regular people began to call him even when they didn't have any work to be done. They would invite him over for lunch so they could look around the house together to find something for him to do!

What can you learn from this Case Study? You must find the people who will become the "right" clients for you where they are spending time. Make it your priority to figure this out and then take massive action to get in front of them.

While I was working as a residential appraiser the time came when the economy was in a slump and I was not getting enough calls from the banks, and mortgage companies to keep me busy. I had to step back and think about the others you could use my services. One group was probate attorneys but I did not know any personally. Then I discovered that they all needed to complete continuing education classes specifically for probate attorneys. It turned out I was able to sign up for these even though I was not an attorney, through my affiliation with the local Board of Realtors.

I showed up on a Saturday morning and introduced myself. There were others there who had real estate licenses and they were hoping to get property listings from the attorneys. I was the only appraiser in attendance and this became a prime source of business for me for years to come. They were looking for certified appraisers with at least five years of experience and who also could complete assignments within seven days. That described me and I offered two references who could verify this. These probate attorneys were even paying a premium price for the appraisals so that was even better for me.

One of my client's works with people who want and need to change the way they are eating in order to gain back their health and quality of life. She intentionally runs into them at the library, the senior center, and especially in the inside aisles of the grocery store. She strikes up a conversation and gives them her card. She is able to answer their questions and her services are one of the solutions to their problem of not being able to enjoy a quality life due to health issues. She is the picture of health and this is in congruence with what she teaches. She also keeps a copy of her bestselling book in her purse to sign and give to prospects when she meets them.

What I am sharing with you here is priceless. Think about the type of people who would be the right clients for you, find out where they are spending time, and then prove to them you are the person they are looking for to complete the tasks they have in mind. Remember that your actions speak louder than words in most cases. This is the Client Attraction Formula that works in helping you to identify, locate, and bring into the fold the right clients for you.

Making the Phone Ring

"Don't be afraid to get creative and experiment with your marketing."
~ Mike Volpe

Early on in my work with local businesses I realized that the goal was to make their phones ring. What happened after that was out of my hands, but getting the phone to ring in the first place was an important first step towards increasing brand awareness and revenue.

Remember that I was a new entrepreneur and business owner in 2006, so I had to put on my thinking cap to figure out marketing strategies that would be effective. As I began to write blog posts, connect with other businesses in forums such as the one on a site called Active Rain, and get out into my new community to meet more people, I came to the realization that I was using myself as a Case Study of sorts for what I would be able to do for my family member and paying clients.

I recommend you do this as well. Think of yourself as someone who is experimenting, learning, course correcting, and moving forward towards a moving target labeled as success. You know that this elusive state of success can be defined in many ways and that success for your business can mean different things to you at various stages of your life and experience owning and running your business.

Begin your Case Study by taking a snapshot of where you are today. This would include Googling your name in quotation marks (I Google for "Connie Ragen Green") to see what the SERPS (search engine results pages) are for you.

This can be tricky if you have a common name like I do. If I Google for "Connie Green" the SERPS include information about a man named Connie Green who was a member of an Irish republican paramilitary group and died the year I was born, as well as information about a former executive chef in northern California, Connie Green. This woman ran a restaurant for a number of years in Napa, California and currently owns an online store. Her specialty is mushrooms and other foraged foods. Her popular book The Wild Table: Seasonal Foraged Food and Recipes was released in 2010 and I'm sure she is as happy as I am that I chose to add my middle name for professional use so that we are not confused with anyone else on the planet.

My first year online Google showed results for Connie the chef on the first couple of pages. When I finally found the two listings for me on page ten or so of Google it didn't matter that one was related to an interview I had done with Parade magazine about violence in the public schools of Los Angeles and the other was a testimonial I had given for a live workshop I had attended on reverse mortgages for seniors. I was just glad to be mentioned.

Once you have found where your name is mentioned on the internet, print out those pages and keep them in a folder for later reference. I honestly wish I had done this in the beginning, as these days there are many thousands of results for my full name, Connie Ragen Green. No one else in the world has my full name, so everything that comes up as a result on Google has something to do with me.

Study the results you find for your name and the name of your business and analyze them as best you can on your own. You are looking for authority sites where you are mentioned. These would include your own and other websites and blogs, social media sites, and articles and/or books you have written and published on the topic of your business.

We will discuss social media in great detail in the next chapter, so for now I only want you to be concerned about having your account set up and profile filled out completely on Twitter, Facebook, and LinkedIn.

The Power of Press Releases

Let's move on to the topic of press releases and how you will be able to leverage the power of reaching the media on demand simply by writing and distributing a short document of several hundred words.

I learned how to write and distribute press releases from an early mentor. These days I send them quite regularly and enjoy the boost in visibility and credibility when I do so. I refer to this marketing strategy as the "Kindergarten Effect." If you have spent any time with a Kindergartner you know they make a big deal out of tiny things.

For example, during one of the two years I taught Kindergarten I had a student named Brandon who was very active and had a short attention span. One day a fly came in through the front door as were returning from recess and Brandon was fixated on this poor insects' every move.

I tried to get the class to settle down so we could get back to our language arts lesson, but Brandon was like an investigative reporter as he announced each move in an informative and dramatic way.

"The fly is on Mrs. Green's desk now!" he squealed.

And just as he leaped on to said desk, scattering my papers in ten different directions the fly moved on to another destination to take refuge and catch its breath, I'm sure.

The idea here is that we as business owners must make a big deal out of everything we do.

Did you start a new blog, or add a post to a blog that has been dormant for a long time? Send a press release.

Just because something feels commonplace to you, or that it would not be of any interest to someone else does not mean that is the case. One time early on someone in my Rotary Club ask me what was new.

"I wrote a blog post this morning," I deadpanned.

You would have thought I had just announced I had been nominated for a Pulitzer Prize!

What was simply part of an ordinary work day for me was a huge deal and great accomplishment to someone outside my business. And a side note here: that same man asked me to write a monthly column for a newspaper he started the following year and I continue to be a columnist to this day. And yes, he has been my marketing client over the years. We share a mutual goal of wanting as many readers as possible for his publication.

Make a list of things that you, your business, or someone who works with you have done that would show your business in a positive light. Plan on sending one press release each month to share these accomplishments with your prospects and customers. Some things to announce would be a new blog or blog post, your products and services, a book you have written, extended or a change to business hours, new location, or a new employee.

You will love it when someone contacts you to compliment you on what you have achieved personally or professionally after they read about it online. Remember to include the "who, what, where, when, and why" in every press release you prepare. There are several sites available where you may send a press release at no cost. These are excellent places for you to practice going through the process from start to finish, but I have found that these press releases seem to disappear very quickly. After you have sent two or three using these free sites, check out a site I have now used for over a decade called WebWire.com. The basic rate is very reasonable and you do not need their more expensive services, in my opinion and based on my experience.

The title of your press release is important and here are some examples that will be effective:

- City/Trade/Industry/Action - Santa Barbara Dentist Announces Evening and Saturday Hours
- City/Resident/Action - Santa Clarita Resident Publishes Book on Local Business Marketing
- Trade/Industry/YourName/Action - Online Marketing Strategist Connie Ragen Green Teaches Virtual Course about Local Business Marketing

The Three-Pronged Approach to Making the Phone Ring

In the fall of 2015 I released a book entitled Book. Blog. Broadcast: The Trifecta of Entrepreneurial Success. I knew the concepts I was sharing were effective, but little did I know how powerful they would prove to be for local businesses. Allow me to explain exactly how this strategy will make a difference for your business.

The three points of the triangle are your book, your blog, and your podcast and videos. I included both podcasts and videos as the "broadcast" piece because they hold equal importance here.

The idea is that you begin by blogging about your business, as I have discussed in earlier chapters. This is the written piece of your marketing and each blog post can be repurposed into social media updates, short reports, white papers, email messages, and a book. Yes, the final piece of this first prong of blogging is to move you closer to outlining your book.

I do realize that asking you to consider writing a book about your business may at first seem like a monumental task. But the truth is that writing a book has never been easier since the world of self-publishing opened up in the early 2000s. As I outlined in Chapter 3, my first book, Huge Profits with a Tiny List: 50 Ways to Use Relationship Marketing to Increase Your Bottom Line began as a simple checklist of ten tips. Using these tips as my starting point I was then able to write ten blog posts and eventually fifty posts were shared on my blog. Over a period of about four months I rewrote each of them and compiled them into my first book. The point I am making here is that if you are able to write five hundred words on any aspect of your business, it is simply a matter of being disciplined enough to accomplish that forty-nine more times in order to have more than enough content for a full length book.

The second prong is focused exclusively on your blog, which I consider to be your "home on the internet." You can add to it once or twice a week yourself, or find someone within your family or your company who will take on this task on your behalf. I prefer to see you as the owner of the business do this yourself so that the book will be written by you, but sharing the authorship with another person is certainly acceptable, especially when you discuss this with them in advance.

Allow your prospects, customers, and clients to interact with you and your company through the blog. Unlike social media platforms, industry forums, and other sites on the internet, your blog is virtual real estate you own and control. This is also where your visitors will be able to opt in to your mailing list and give you permission to stay in touch with them in this way. This was a favorite mode of communication for the HVAC company I marketed for several years ago and they have continued to blog regularly.

The third and final prong is broadcasting, which encompasses both audio and video marketing. You may begin with audio recordings or teleseminars, where you share information about your business with those who are interested in learning more about you and your topic. The idea here is to finally start a podcast where your audio messages may be found by people all over the world when they do a keyword search. The plumbers I marketed for loved this part and could talk endlessly on topics around plumbing and pipes.

Broadcasting also includes videos. I recommend using YouTube and Vimeo simultaneously for best results. Keep all videos to under five minutes in length and remember you are marketing to people who have both an interest as well as a problem around your topic and area of expertise.

As you become more comfortable and proficient with all three prongs, the next step is to play each of them individually off the other two. What I mean by this is that you will include information about your blog on your videos and podcast, you will mention your videos on your podcast and blog, and so forth. The culmination of your blog content into a book allows you to discuss your blog, videos, and podcast within its pages and you will have come full circle. The idea is to make sure that anyone who encounters any one of your prongs will soon have knowledge of everything else you are doing.

Social media can be updated throughout each day by a virtual assistant to allow your target audience to choose the method they prefer when it comes to getting to know more about you and your topic.

Making the phone ring is all about rising above the competition and distancing yourself from them whenever possible. At some point you will acknowledge that you have no competitors, only colleagues with whom you engage in something referred to as coopetition. This is the place you arrive at once you are able to cooperatively compete with others in your field so that you each attract the right clients and customers and there is plenty of work to go around as all businesses rise at the rate and to the level desired by the business owner.

Some excellent ways to rise above all others in your industry is by writing a book, becoming a public speaker, and teaching at the local adult school or community college. From local to nationwide to international you will quickly become a sought after expert who is able to write their own ticket when it comes to expanding your business.

Social Media

"Build it, and they will come" only works in the movies.
Social Media is a "build it, nurture it, engage them, and they
may come and stay."
~ Seth Godin

I began my business during the dark ages, at least according to some sources. In 2006 Facebook was still for college students. Even though I was in graduate school at the time and had the required .edu email address extension, in my memory I did not hear anything about this site until two years later. Twitter was not created until 2008. The way people connected on the internet was through something called bulletin boards. This gave us a sense of community that would eventually lead to social media sites like Facebook, Twitter, and an updated version of LinkedIn.

Bulletin boards were a challenge to maneuver at times but gave us a way to ask questions and share our thoughts and opinions on specific topics of interest with others. A Bulletin Board System or BBS (once called Computer Bulletin Board Service, CBBS) is a computer server running software that allows users to connect to the system using a terminal program. Once logged in, the user can perform functions such as uploading and downloading software and data, reading news and bulletins, and exchanging messages with other users through public message boards and sometimes via direct chatting. I was aware of bulletin boards in the early 1980s. They included something that would be the precursor to email.

Then CompuServe appeared at some point in the late 1980s, assigning us each a number instead of our name. AOL appeared in 1991, giving us a choice as to how we would move forward in the information age with our own identity and ability to communicate. When they launched their "Instant Messenger" program in '91 AOL changed how I perceived the future of my own interpersonal communications. I would send a message from my computer to that of a friend's, call them on the phone to see if they had received it, and then we would talk for the next twenty minutes or so about topics of great importance and little significance. You were allowed one message per day or thirty each month. No one could ever imagine needing more than this when you could now telephone people all over the world without needing an international operator's assistance. Even though I was connecting to the internet at a slower than a snail's pace speed it was a huge improvement over the old system and procedure on the bulletin boards.

Once dial up connections became more affordable and web browsers like Mosaic were invented most of the BBSes closed down. This was in the late 1980s and I still remember the clumsy process of connecting to a bulletin board via a 300 baud Smartmodem to chat with students in my graduate courses at the university I was enrolled in to complete my teacher credential program. That modem made the weirdest sounds as it chugged along to make the connection. If you were online at this time you can most likely hear those sounds as you are reading this section. I went from 300 baud to 1200 and finally to 2400 baud. Dial up internet service was made widely available in 1994 and soon modems were something you kept as a souvenir of forgotten times.

With the speed of everything computer related during that decade (the 90s) it is surprising to me that it took so long for social sites like Facebook to finally appear in 2003.

Myspace was actually the first social media site, even though it was originally intended to be a way for artists and musicians to share their work with the world. Between the years of 2005 and 2009 it was the largest social media network in the world. Facebook began to overtake them in the Alexa rankings as early as 2008 and Myspace began to decrease in membership, slowly at first and then more rapidly as people in the mainstream flocked to Facebook. As a part of my research for this book I discovered that I still had an account with Myspace and logged in to see what was there. It was a blast from the past.

LinkedIn had already been in business since 2003 but it was geared towards people in the corporate world as a directory of sorts. I mentioned earlier that I did sign up for LinkedIn around 2007 and was mortified when they went through my email connections (I clicked an incorrect button; they did nothing wrong) and immediately invitations were sent out to everyone I knew in my Rotary Club. I considered staying home the day of our next meeting but went anyway to face the music. Imagine my surprise when several people came up and shook my hand and congratulated me for connecting with them on LinkedIn. While I hadn't felt worthy because of my status as a new online entrepreneur, the other Rotarians considered me to be an equal.

By 2008 we had entered a new realm with social media. It was going mainstream quickly and paid advertising possibilities made Madison Avenue and Wall Street take notice. It was a modern day version of Mad Men, with people all over the world fixated and possessed over what the outcome could be in financial terms. When Facebook Ads launched in 2007 even small entrepreneurs like myself stood up and took notice. Any company could now purchase advertising on the Facebook platform with relative ease. Initially all ads were relegated to a new column of the far right hand side of the Facebook Newsfeed for reasons unknown, but that soon changed. Google's AdWords program, first available in 2000 was no longer the only game in town.

And it wasn't only advertising executives, stock brokers, and content creators who were salivating over these new social platforms. It was people like me, entrepreneurs and marketers who could imagine the future where everything could be shared online within these public forums. I continue to recommend that small businesses begin with free social media campaigns before employing paid ones.

As for small business owners I know and work with, the overwhelming majority of them continue to miss out on the power of social media marketing. They joke about not caring what someone ate for breakfast or what a celebrity is wearing. So when I hear that kind of talk I remain silent until they are finished talking and then I lean in closer and say something like:

"I know social media seems silly to most people. But I'm grateful to have a simple way to reach a mass audience and find new prospects and clients without having to spend any money on advertising. That could save you many thousands of dollars each month and it only takes a few hours a week to implement."

Then I take a small step back and look away from the person I am speaking with. Next, I open my purse as if I am searching for my phone or something else and excuse myself. I walk away slowly, counting in my head...

Depending upon how long it takes for my words to land on the business owner's eardrum, translate into their brain, and finally connect to their vocal chords so they have a voice in order for them to respond to my comment, we soon have scheduled a time to speak further on this topic. Yes, I adamant about sharing what I know with others and unwavering in my efforts to spread marketing strategies with those who will listen, implement, and benefit from my expertise.

Let's look at each on the "Big Three" of social media - Twitter, Facebook, and LinkedIn one by one.

Twitter

"Tweet, tweet" said the little bird and my life was changed forever. It was April of 2008 and I was enthralled with the idea of telling the world what I was doing in one hundred forty characters or less.

Because I was early to this platform I was able to secure the handle @ConnieGreen. Connie Ragen Green was one character too long so no one else would have it either. I squatted on @ConnieRGreen for awhile and gave it up at some point.

Twitter doubled our pleasure in November of 2017 and as of his writing we now have two hundred eighty characters at our disposal for each tweet. I personally believe this was done for political reasons and if everyone benefits as a result, so be it.

I think of a tweet as a headline so I capitalize each word of my title. Then I give a description of my blog post, course, or product I am sharing, followed by the link to the site where the viewer can learn more. This has similarities to classified advertisements. If you have ever made a study of classifieds as I have done, you will take to Twitter quickly and enjoy excellent results.

Choose a "handle" that makes sense for your location and industry, if at all possible. For example, there is a periodontist in Ventura, California who goes by the Twitter handle of @VenturaGumGuy. He also understands the value of adding what is known as hash tags to his social media updates. He has used #periodontist, #periodontaldisease and #dentalimpants most recently to make it easier for anyone searching for these topics to locate him more easily.

Facebook

Facebook was the brainchild of Mark Zuckerberg while he was a student at Harvard. Most of what occurred in those first few years has now become a part of our culture and history so I will only share the highlights here. Zuckerberg launched Facebook, first as Facemash and next as Thefacebook from his dormitory room on February 4, 2004, with his college roommates Eduardo Saverin, Andrew McCollum, Dustin Moskovitz, and Chris Hughes. They originally intended to only launch this new social media platform to select college campuses, specifically Stanford, Yale, and Columbia. The site expanded rapidly, reaching one million users by December of 2015, and eventually beyond college boundaries, reaching one billion users by 2012. Zuckerberg took the company public in May 2012 with majority shares.

There are multiple opportunities for small businesses to expand their reach and increase market share on Facebook. Start by creating a business page in the name of your company and asking your Facebook friends to "like" it as a way of growing your following.

I recommend building a following on your personal page (your wall) and then inviting them over to the business page you have created.

LinkedIn

LinkedIn began as an idea in late 2002 and launched to the world in 2003. As of this writing they are approaching six hundred million users, with a third of these active on any given day.

Even though this social media platform had no interest in becoming one, I believe they have made significant changes to the site over the past decade due to pressure from Facebook.

I find LinkedIn to be the perfect platform for businesses. You have access to the people who are, in my opinion more focused and serious about business and life in general than those frequenting almost any other social site.

Right now there is a limit of thirty thousand first level connections and I am approaching that number rapidly. This gives me a distinct advantage in that I am able to directly reach out to almost anyone in the world who is also a LinkedIn user.

As a business owner you may want to reach out to others in your field for ideas, masterminds, and friendship. I have helped people in real estate and in the health and wellness community in this respect and it has been beneficial for them in a variety of ways. Imagine getting a fellow dentist in another state on the phone to ask about their experience with a new procedure. LinkedIn makes sense for all types of businesses.

Instagram, YouTube, and Pinterest

These three social media sites are also worth your time. I am grouping them together as ways to separate them from the "big three" so that you will make the sites that are, in my opinion most advantageous to small business growth your priority right now.

Also, find someone within your company or a freelancer to set up or update your profiles and to come up with an initial plan to get things moving for you.

Thought Leaders

What I love most about social media is how we are all on equal footing, at least to some degree when we send out our posts and updates. At any given point in time any one of us may tweet or post something that has the potential to change the world. The down side of this ability to communicate with millions or even a billions human beings is that we may never know what we shared that made such a huge impact on another person so that we may use that information strategically.

Begin to think of yourself as a thought leader within your industry and demonstrate this through the power of social media. Start within your community, gather a following of people interested in what you have to say, and then run with it over time on a consistent basis. I've done this for myself, as well as for plumbers, dentists, chiropractors, and other business owners in the service trades and professional services. We are all looking for honest advice, proven strategies, and people we can look up to in various areas of our lives.

You will be amazed at how quickly your prospects and potential customers and clients will resonate with your knowledge, experience, and expertise in specific areas and will resonate in a way that makes sense for everyone.

Lead Generation

Generating leads from social media can be done in one of two ways. The first method includes building relationships with people you know away from social media and inviting them to "like" your business page. Then you take them through a funnel where they are able to learn more about you and what your business has to offer. If they are a prospect you will take them away from Facebook and back to your blog and website where they will have the chance to connect with your company and take the next steps to do business with you.

The second strategy involves running a series of paid advertisements on Facebook and creating "audiences" of people who may be excellent prospects, based on a series of criteria. There are several paths to take here and you want to be careful as you spend money here and document everything you do in a step by step manner.

I am oversimplifying here in the interest of allowing you to come to your own conclusions as to how this will work best for you. Without having a personal consultation with you about how to proceed I do not want to take the chance that you will be misled or that something I write here will change significantly once the book goes to press. My apologies if this is not what you want to hear and please know there are people available that can better serve you with cutting edge, relevant, and current details on this topic. Contact me for more detailed information and recommendations.

Section Five – What's Next?

> "Leverage the strength that you have: that no one else can be you."
> ~ Todd Wheatland

You now have a better idea of what it takes to market your business in a way that will increase your bottom line. Go back and reread any sections where you feel like you need additional help or information. If you have the paperback version of this book, underline and add sticky notes where needed. If you have a digital copy use the highlight feature to mark important passages. Internalize ideas and strategies to use as soon as possible. Although each chapter of this book is intended to stand on its own, you may wish to reread it in its entirety, or at least review each section as you are working through the principles and strategies I have included and expounded upon.

Take it upon yourself to contact me or to seek out other local business marketing experts who can take you closer to where you want your business to be, for both the short and long run. Do not take no for an answer if anyone tells you something cannot be done. That simply is not true.

Now think about the direction you wish to head after reading through this book again, making some detailed notes, and researching further online and off. This is only a resting point as you catapult your way to success in a direction that makes sense for you. An early mentor, Armand Morin taught me to always know the next logical step in the process of moving forward with my goals and dreams. It was not necessary for me to know or understand everything I would need for years into the future, as long as I knew what came next that week or month.

The Two Directions That May Seem Like the Next Logical Steps for You Are:
1) Becoming an expert in marketing for your own business and/or
2) Marketing for other small businesses as a consultant

Having done both of these for well over a decade now I will tell you that you do not need to become an expert at marketing your own business before becoming a consultant to other small businesses. In fact, your business will benefit greatly if you begin working with other business owners. I believe this is due to the fact that we think differently when we are wearing different hats. As a business owner I tend to have blinders on when it comes to some marketing strategies and only think "out of the box" when specific situations arise; as a small business consultant I am more open to this style of "out of the box" thinking on a daily basis.

Also, you may find yourself more motivated to go above and beyond for someone else when working to improve their systems and increase their bottom line in a way you are not as likely to do for your own business. This may not describe your work ethic and personality at all but I wanted to share that we all tend to act and serve differently when someone else's welfare is in our hands.

Marketing for Other Businesses

"You can have everything you want in life if you just help enough people get what they want in life."
~ Zig Ziglar

One disadvantage I have as an author is the lack of ability to know who is reading my books. You may be a new entrepreneur, an owner of a small business, or someone who wishes to market for other entrepreneurs and small businesses. I am working blind when I speak to an audience that is unknown to me so I will do my best to include every possible detail and scenario in this chapter.

Up until this point I have been speaking to the first two above - entrepreneurs and small business owners. Now I will address the third group, marketers for small businesses they do not own or run or have a vested interest in, personally or financially.

I shared many of my own experiences in this area of marketing for local businesses throughout the book. I recommend you go back and review those chapters, especially if you looked through the table of contents and skipped ahead to this chapter. It is always tempting to skip to what you may consider to be the "good part" of a book without having to wade through many pages of information that you believe is not relevant to your personal goals, but that is risky and may minimize your success in the long run.

Please do not shortchange yourself in this way. I was strategic in how this book was put together and unfolds for your ultimate benefit. In my efforts to serve two audiences I made sure to tell the story of local business marketing in its entirety. I implore you to read this entire book for maximum results, and in a way that will allow you to be productive in the shortest space of time.

Marketing for Businesses is a Worthwhile Pursuit

What I am about to share with here is the strategy and business model I used to reach an annual six figure income during my first year as an online entrepreneur. In the process of going offline to help small businesses and during the worst recession since the Great Depression I learned enough to build my own business to seven figures within a five year period. It required hard work and dedication on my part, and you will benefit from the mistakes and missteps that occurred over a period of years as I refined the proven method that I continue to use and teach to this day. Yes, I have an online course that teaches everything I am sharing with you here in this chapter, and in much greater detail than I am able to go into here. Start with this and then contact me if you are interested in the online training and in working more closely with me.

Laying Your Foundation

You will first want to familiarize yourself with WordPress, the website platform I discussed in detail in the third chapter. Having the ability to discuss this topic intelligently and with the voice of confidence and authority with your prospects and clients is crucial to your success.

This conversation will come early on and gives you the opportunity to show them you are someone they can trust to help them achieve their goals.

Set up a few WordPress sites of your own to learn from and practice with to explore and discover the possibilities. One of these will be your main website for attracting new prospects and clients and you want it to showcase your ongoing knowledge and implementation of what a website can do for business owners.

Next comes SEO (search engine optimization) so you will be able to leverage, and to some extent control how you and your clients will be seen, perceived, and found on the internet. I find the whole SEO process to be a fascinating one that morphs over time. Keeping up with these ongoing changes can be a challenge, but one that will pay off as your knowledge and abilities increase and improve.

Imagine being able to make a post to a website and have it cone up in the SERPS (search engine results pages) within fifteen minutes or so.

Finally, content creation and syndication is a necessary skill to master and one that can benefit you and your clients by giving you an almost unfair advantage in the marketplace.

Once your foundation is in place you are ready to move on to the next step.

Where Are They Right Now in Their Businesses?

The easiest way to find out where someone's business is at the current moment when it comes to visibility and credibility is to do some quick research on Google. Begin with the name of the owner of the business and use quotation marks around their name. Next, Google their industry and city in which the business is located.

For example, if I am going after a prospect named Doug Sutton who runs a classified magazine in Santa Clarita I would first Google "doug sutton" and then Google "magazine santa clarita."

Upon doing so I would discover that Doug runs a newspaper called the Gazette and that he and his wife are in a legal dispute with another newspaper called The Signal. He is also a Rotarian and a member of the Santa Clarita Business Group.

From the SERPs (search engine results pages) that are returned by Google I see immediately that I must also Google for "santa clarita newspaper" in order to find all of the information I need. When I do so there are several more newspapers and magazines based in Santa Clarita that are important to this process.

Now it's time to print out the first two pages for each search you just conducted. I did three searches and would print out six pages in all. Add this to a folder that you will have with you when you meet with your prospect in person.

Positioning Yourself as the Solution

Choose a quiet place to meet with your prospect. Coffee shops, restaurants, and other public places will not allow you to control the environment and to present yourself in the best light. The prospect's office could be even more distracting because the owner of the business is typically in high demand when they are present.

Instead, set an appointment with them at their home or at your home or office. If their spouse or business partner is also a decision maker, be sure to include them. During my first years working in real estate I made the mistake more than once of meeting with only one of the decision makers and was unable to take the listing on the property or write an offer after showing several properties because the other person was not present at the time. Learn from my mistakes and find out in advance who is responsible for making the decision to work with you on marketing their business.

When you are finally together in quiet surroundings make some small talk for a few minutes and then take out the folder you have prepared for them. Ask them if they know the business owners and the businesses that appear on page one of Google. They most likely do. Gently place in their hands the pages you have printed out where those names appear.

Then give them a couple of minutes to respond. Be kind and listen as they tell you their story. All business owners have a story they share when they are being open and transparent with someone who may be able to help them. In their mind it is similar to you being a banker or an investment advisor who could make a difference for them with a business loan. But what you have to offer is of much greater value because you have the power to make their phone ring and bring them more business.

Show them what you have done for your own business and for that of a close friend or family member. In my case I was still in the process of adding more credibility and visibility to my business. I had also experienced great success and results with the handyman I had been marketing for over the past couple of months and one other client that had just come aboard the previous month.

I did not pretend to have more experience than I actually did at that time. When you are honest in your dealings with others they are much more likely to work with you. This also sets the tone for how you will do everything in your life, whether it is for business or personal reasons.

While I was sitting in the living room of the home of my dentist and his wife I literally laid it all out on the table. We were also in Rotary together and I had taken on the role of Chair of the Marketing and Public Relations Committee just months earlier. Based on what I had been able to accomplish for myself, my family member, an insurance agent they also knew, and our Rotary Club the dentist and his wife agreed to have me help them. We shook on a six month contract and I spelled out the minimum I would do for them each week, after the initial setup. I had adequately positioned myself as the solution to their problem and gained a new client.

Make a list of why you are the right solution to the marketing challenges faced by your prospect. Read your list aloud and talk in front of a full length mirror. Stand up straight and tall and be aware of your body language. Be confident in your abilities to help small businesses to make their phones ring.

"Local" Does Not Mean Local to You

For one thing, know that the small businesses you will be helping will not all be local to you. One of my early clients who embraced this business model and did extremely well coming out the gate was the person who pointed this out to me.

Helen and her husband were living in a high rise condominium in downtown Toronto when I first met them online. He had a job with an international corporation based there and they had relocated from Michigan so he would not have to commute. Helen had decided to start a coaching business she could run from anywhere in the world. When she took one of my trainings on local business marketing she was sure this would be an excellent addition to her entrepreneurial goals. I guided her through the process of attracting and signing up the right clients for her, helping with the initial setup, and then through the process of making their phones rings. For some reason I just assumed all of her clients were located in Toronto and the surrounding areas of Ontario.

The following year we met in person for the first time at a large marketing event in Los Angeles. The first evening we went up to the concierge level to have some private time to talk.

Imagine my surprise when Helen told me all nine of her clients were in the States! When I asked her how this happened she explained that she had connected with people from a service organization she had spent time volunteering with more than a decade earlier. She had always been a social person and an excellent networker so this came natural to her. When she had announced her new business model to this group via email, social media, and some personal phone calls the right clients for her had come aboard.

Be creative and do what it takes to make this business of helping other small businesses work for you.

Setting Up a Business Initially

You have taken on a small business client and have made promises you intend to keep. What do you do first? Next? On an ongoing basis? Let's take a look at what marketing for local businesses entails.

The first step is to determine your specific goals for your new client. This is done with them and any members of their team who may wish to be included. When I set up the insurance agent as a client his office manager was involved. The same was true for the dentist. With the plumbers I marketed for, it was their Google AdWords and SEO manager who was located in Australia.

Once an initial plan is written out in detail it's time for you to get to work. The activities included would be:

- Setting up a Gmail account for the client so that you may sign up for what you will be setting up for them. The client has full access to this email account.
- Purchasing domain names to be used for the new WordPress sites you will be setting up. Typically these would include the city and the industry, such as "Dallas plumbers." Doing this in reverse - "plumbers Dallas" may be necessary if the original is already taken.
- Setting up a hosting account for the client. I recommend the company I am using currently, through my affiliate link. I should note here that the client owns and controls the accounts with the domain registrar and the hosting company. I have access to these in order to do the work required, but the goal is for the business owner to be able to take over at some point in the future. This is the ethical, preferred manner of doing business.
- Setting up and/or managing social media accounts on behalf of your client. Again, these accounts belong to the business owner and you will have full access to them while you are working on their behalf.
- Setting up and maintaining one or more WordPress sites for them.
- Creating content that would include blog posts, social media updates, press releases, short reports, white papers

Another thing I'd like to note here is that you will only want to take on two new clients each month, at least for the first two months. This is because the setup and tasks for each client will take longer in the beginning and you don't want to overwhelm yourself or shortchange your new clients by taking on too much. By the third month you will have more experience and know what to expect and that is when you can fill your calendar with additional clients to reach the maximum you can take care of yourself before deciding to take on freelancers and outsourcers.

Your First Free Client

I accidentally discovered that by helping the handyman, a family member, for a couple of months before taking on a paid client that this was the preferred sequence of events. Even if you have been successful in marketing your own business it is beneficial to build your credibility based on your results for another business before asking someone to invest their time and money with you.

This gives you at least thirty days to increase the visibility of the person you are helping so that you may share your results with potential paying clients. It is possible to accomplish quite a bit during a full month of marketing, engaging in the activities I mentioned above.

You may be wondering where you will find this first free client. My recommendation is to make a list of close friends and family members who already have a business and are not paying for advertising at the present time. These are the people who will most benefit from what you will be able to achieve for them in terms of giving them the visibility that is needed in order to make their phone ring.

Once you have half a dozen names on your list reach out personally to each person and schedule a time to meet with them. Explain that you have been marketing for your own business and learning as much as you can. Show and tell them some examples of how you have increased your credibility and visibility and what you results have been so far since you began.

Then tell them you would like to offer this set of skills to business owners as a paid service. Explain that you would like to do this for them at no cost, except for the cost of some domain names and a web hosting account. They will own the domains and control the hosting account and when the time comes that you will not be serving them in this capacity any longer there will be a smooth transition. Explain the value of this arrangement and how it will be mutually beneficial.

Answer the questions they have and determine if this is the right person to take on as your free client. If so, shake hands on the deal for a six month period, after which you will meet with them to evaluate the effectiveness of your efforts and to determine if you will continue marketing on their behalf for your usual monthly fee.

If this is not the right person for you, thank them for their time and move on to the next person on your list. What you are offering here has great value. You want to make sure your efforts are appreciated and that this client will make an excellent case study as you move forward in your new business.

Earning Your Keep

You must work hard to serve your small business clients. You will work the longest and the hardest during your first two months with each business because there is so much to set up and put in motion. This includes the blog(s), social media profiles, and the SEO (search engine optimization) words and phrases you will optimize for to achieve the best results.

I would wait until the beginning of the second month to set up a YouTube channel with videos you have created with your smart phone. Then it's time to add Instagram and perhaps Pinterest. I prefer to shoot a dozen videos within a few hours and then drip them out on YouTube over the next several months.

Make sure your client knows what you are doing. This can be achieved with a weekly email update. When I began working for the first dentist I was very excited when his original website, one created from a template by the Yellow Pages had finally moved from page seventy-eight (yes, I went through Google page by page until I located it) to page two on Google. He and his wife were in Dallas at a dental seminar that week so I created a short video showing what I had been able to do and emailed the link to them. When they returned they told me they had watched the video together in their hotel room and it had been one of the highlights of their trip.

Work diligently during the first month or two and you will be in a position to serve all of your clients in an excellent manner from day to day.

Teaching Marketing to Others

"Those who know, do. Those that understand, teach."
~ Aristotle

I have talked about the two plumbers I marketed for throughout this book. We met on a flight from Los Angeles to Atlanta in April of 2008. By the time we touched down at Hartsfield-Jackson we had scribbled a contract on a cocktail napkin that would last for two years, earn me more than fifty thousand dollars, and help them create a plumbing empire in southern California that did not require them to be there in person for months at a time.

Now I can't take all the credit for their success; they were well on their way to creating an eight figure business when I entered the picture. I was a piece of their marketing puzzle and learned much from them during our years working together in this capacity. I was also able to observe firsthand as they went from being ambitious to thinking bigger than they ever could have imagined.

I watched as they took advantage of every opportunity that presented itself. In 2010 they attended a convention for business owners in the service trades. This annual event was held in Chicago and it was the first time they had attended. During this event something occurred that positioned them in a unique way to the audience.

There was a keynote speaker who called on people to share how they were sharing their expertise with others. One of my plumbers raised his hand and answered that he was in a mastermind of business owners and was sharing with them how the strategies he was using could help another member who was struggling with his printing business.

The speaker cut him off mid sentence and he was quickly ushered to the stage and handed a microphone. Over the next ten minutes he answered questions from the speaker and then audience members about how something that worked in the plumbing industry could also work for businesses that focused on painting, electrical, printing, HVAC (heating, ventilation, and air conditioning) as well as for other plumbers.

As they related this story to me they described it as being surreal and that at some point everything around them was in slow motion. Then they simultaneously had an epiphany that changed their lives forever. Instead of simply building a plumbing business with over a hundred physical locations that was increasing in revenue every single month they could also begin teaching others plumbers and other trades how they were achieving the results that were working for them so consistently.

This would be a new business that now made sense to both of them. Instead of simply working as plumbers and running a plumbing company they would now be teaching and consulting with owners of businesses in the trades.

It took them six months to plan everything out. Then they chose a test market in the Houston, Texas area because that is where they both lived with their families. That's right; they built a billion dollar empire more than fifteen hundred miles (about 2500 km) from home.

A year later I invited them to a marketing conference in Las Vegas. It was hosted by a man who is still considered to be one of the foremost experts in the marketing space and someone I had learned from over several years. I had told him about the success the plumbers were experiencing and he wanted to meet them.

I was so proud as they took the stage in front of over a thousand attendees to answer questions about their business. They were confident and excited to share what I and others had done to help them create their dream business and lifestyle. By the end of that day they were celebrities and many people wanted to learn from them. They were even invited to go to downtown Las Vegas in a chauffeur driven stretch limousine!

Teaching marketing to small business owners is a worthwhile endeavor. A marketing strategy or application you take for granted is pure genius when explained to another business owner. Think of it as sharing proven principles to others who would benefit from learning about marketing from you. This is what I do every day in my work as an online marketing strategist, but it has only recently been applicable to the offline world. And I believe we have only seen the tip of the iceberg when it comes to changing the face of business consulting to include the trades as well as the professions and in a way that embraces teaching what you know to one or a small group of business owners.

This work is satisfying and rewarding. Imagine working with two or three business owners who are new to your industry and anxious to learn as much as they can to better compete in the marketplace. Long ago this was the relationship between an apprentice and a journeyman. These days we have informal mentoring and I have experienced that many times now since becoming an entrepreneur, but it is now quite the same thing.

Of course this is an optional part of your journey. You may be perfectly content with building your business to a greater level of success by implementing what I have shared throughout this book. But I wanted to at least expose you to what is possible when you are willing to reach higher, think bigger, and help more people. Growing to achieve specific, measurable goals will always be in vogue.

Summary/Conclusion

It was six men of Indostan
To learning much inclined,
Who went to see the Elephant
(Though all of them were blind),
That each by observation
Might satisfy his mind.

First Verse of "The Blind Men and the Elephant"
~ John Godfrey Saxe

You may be familiar with the parable of the blind men and the elephant. This originated in southern India. It goes like this:

A group of blind men heard that a strange animal, called an elephant, had been brought to the town, but none of them were aware of its shape and form. Out of curiosity, they said: "We must inspect and know it by touch, of which we are capable." So, they sought it out, and when they found it they groped about it.

In the case of the first person, whose hand landed on the trunk, said "This being is like a thick snake." For another one whose hand reached its ear, it seemed like a kind of fan. As for another person, whose hand was upon its leg, said, the elephant is a pillar like a tree-trunk. The blind man who placed his hand upon its side said the elephant, "is a wall." Another who felt its tail, described it as a rope. The last felt its tusk, stating the elephant is that which is hard, smooth and like a spear.

In some versions of this parable, the blind men soon discover their disagreements, accuse the others of not being honest, and come to blows. The stories also differ primarily in how the elephant's body parts are described, how violent the conflict becomes and how (or if) the conflict among the men and their perspectives is resolved. In some versions, they stop talking, start listening and collaborate to "see" the full elephant. In another, a sighted man enters the parable and describes the entire elephant from various perspectives, the blind men then learn that they were all partially correct and partially wrong. While one's subjective experience is true, it may not be the totality of truth.

When I think of local business marketing, this parable always comes to mind. Marketing represents one thing to one person, and something very different to another. Yes, you can measure your results based on your bottom line, but the target of marketing success is one that continues to move as you redefine and then further refine what it means to you.

As you begin or continue to market for your own business, and/or for other small business owners, remember that you are responsible for the actions and efforts you take each day. Start from where you are right now and make a plan to move forward to get closer to your goals.

Remember what I stated early on in this book; I believe small businesses in the States will benefit greatly from small business owners learning more about marketing and taking responsibility in this area. The results will include increased revenue, improved relationships with other business owners and the community, and the ability to stay in business over a longer period of time. It will make an even greater difference as the economy ebbs and flows rhythmically over time. The only way to enjoy these benefits is to educate yourself about marketing and to make a conscious shift in your thinking as to how you will be able to use what you learn to make your phone ring more regularly.

Review the history of marketing and advertising and how we moved into modern times based on where we came from in the first two chapters. Hindsight is 20/20 and having the ability to learn from the people, concepts, and strategies that set the stage for what we are able to accomplish in modern times is a goldmine waiting to be tapped.

Take copious notes as you reread what I have included in this book, and know that you and I will disagree more often than not on the strategies, tactics, and methods I have shared. I welcome the opportunity to discuss with you anything I have included here and to learn from you and your own unique experiences.

About the Author

Wouldn't take nothing for my journey now.
~ Maya Angelou

Connie Ragen Green is an online marketing strategist, bestselling author, international speaker, and mentor to people on six continents. A former classroom teacher, real estate broker, and residential appraiser, she left it all behind to start an online business during 2006.

This change of direction with career, lifestyle, and goals occurred as she came to realize that she wanted something more from her life than what she was currently experiencing. This was the beginning of a new life, where anything is possible and everything unfolds in a magical way.

After struggling during her first year of entrepreneurship, Connie finally embraced these struggles of writing and technology, leveled up her work ethic, carefully chose her mentors, and continues to exceed her own potential in her life and business.

Making her home in two cities, Santa Barbara, California at the beach and Santa Clarita, California in the desert, Connie is active with a number of charities, non-profits, and service organizations. These include Rotary, an international service organization; Zonta, a women's business organization with the Mission of advancing the status of women worldwide; the Benevolent and Protective Order of Elk; the Boys and Girls Clubs of America; and SEE International, an organization dedicated to restoring the vision of people in underdeveloped countries. In 2016 she was chosen as the recipient of the Merrill Hoffman Award for her dedication to service for people in need.

She hosts live marketing events twice a year in the Los Angeles, California area, as well as hosting small group Retreats in Santa Barbara several times each year.

Becoming an online entrepreneur changed Connie's life forever. Once she became versed in online marketing and observed first-hand how powerful the effect was for people all over the world, she began writing on a variety of topics, creating information products, speaking at live events and workshops, and mentoring people on how to build a successful and lucrative business they can run from home or from anywhere in the world. She also works with corporations in the area of online marketing and sales strategies.

Find out more and receive some relevant information right away by visiting https://ConnieRagenGreen.com to further connect with Connie and to begin your own journey of online entrepreneurship.

www.ingramcontent.com/pod-product-compliance
Lightning Source LLC
Chambersburg PA
CBHW060615210326
41520CB00010B/1341